Elite • 262

American Civil War Amphibious Tactics

Seamen, Ordinary Seamen,
BOATMEN, LANDSMEN,
MECHANICS, AND OTHERS,
WANTED FOR THE
MARINE ARTILLERY,
W. A. HOWARD, Colonel, Commanding,
Now in active service in
GEN. BURNSIDE'S EXPEDITION.
Pay the same as the Navy, and $100 bounty at the expiration of term of service, which is three years or the war. Allotment tickets to secure half pay can be left for families, or any member thereof, payable on each pay-day, in New-York. The Colonel will issue certificates to the families of those joining, entitling them to the benefits of the Volunteer Fund in New-York and Brooklyn. The men will also receive a neat and comfortable outfit, bed and bedding, on being mustered in. A few good FIFERS and DRUMMERS are needed. Early application is necessary, to M. O'MALLEY, No. 78 Bowery, between Canal and Hester-sts., N. Y.

RON FIELD

ILLUSTRATED BY STEVE NOON
Series editors Martin Windrow & Nick Reynolds

OSPREY PUBLISHING
Bloomsbury Publishing Plc
Kemp House, Chawley Park, Cumnor Hill, Oxford OX2 9PH, UK
Bloomsbury Publishing Ireland Limited,
29 Earlsfort Terrace, Dublin 2, D02 AY28, Ireland
1385 Broadway, 5th Floor, New York, NY 10018, USA
E-mail: info@ospreypublishing.com
www.ospreypublishing.com

OSPREY is a trademark of Osprey Publishing Ltd

First published in Great Britain in 2025

A catalog record for this book is available from the British Library.

ISBN: PB 9781472863164; eBook 9781472863171;
ePDF 9781472863140; XML 9781472863157

25 26 27 28 29 10 9 8 7 6 5 4 3 2 1

Index by Rob Munro
Typeset by PDQ Digital Media Solutions, Bungay, UK
Printed and bound in India by Repro India Ltd.

Osprey Publishing supports the Woodland Trust, the UK's leading woodland
conservation charity.

To find out more about our authors and books visit
www.ospreypublishing.com. Here you will find extracts, author
interviews, details of forthcoming events and the option to sign up for
our newsletter.

For product safety related questions contact productsafety@bloomsbury.com

Acknowledgments

The author wishes to thank John "J-Cat" Griffith, Dennis Hood, and Paul
Russinoff for their generous assistance.

Artist's note

Readers may care to note that the original paintings from which the color
plates in this book were prepared are available for private sale. All
reproduction copyright whatsoever is retained by the publishers. All
enquiries should be addressed to:

https://www.steve-noon.co.uk/

The publishers regret that they can enter into no correspondence upon
this matter.

Title-page illustration: Recruitment notice published in the *New York
Daily Tribune* (*NYDT*, February 15, 1862: 1.3), offering a bounty of $100
to encourage volunteers, particularly with sea service, to enlist in the
1st New York Marine Artillery. (Author's collection)

CONTENTS

AMERICAN CIVIL WAR AMPHIBIOUS TACTICS

INTRODUCTION

Based on a painting by Lieutenant Henry A. Walke, USN, and published by Sarony & Major, 117 Fulton Street, New York City, this lithograph depicts the landing of US soldiers, sailors, and Marines in the Tabasco River near San Juan Bautista, Mexico, on March 9, 1847, during the Mexican–American War. (Library of Congress LC-DIG-pga-04091)

With the outbreak of the Civil War in April 1861, it became obvious to Northern military commanders that amphibious assaults at strategic points along the Atlantic coastline, and inland on the Great Rivers of the Midwest, would be required in order to subjugate the rebellious Southern States. Although amphibious warfare by the US Navy and Army formed part of previous American military experience, the tactics involved required further development to meet the demands of improving technology in the context of a much wider conflict.

The Marines of the Continental Navy made ship-to-shore landings on New Providence Island, Bahamas, in 1776, and at Penobscot Bay, Maine, in 1779. Although largely unopposed, the successful landings in the Tabasco

River near San Juan Bautista, Mexico, of US Army soldiers and US Navy sailors and Marines, under Commodore Matthew C. Perry, on March 9, 1847, during the Mexican–American War (1846–48) had involved 50 ships carrying 15,000 troops plus a large siege train. In 1856, during the Second Opium War (1856–60), 287 sailors and Marines landed and systematically captured all four "Barrier Forts" in the Pearl River, China, in response to the Chinese firing on boats from the sloop-of-war *Portsmouth*. Although these various landings were successful, the challenges facing the US military on land and at sea during the Civil War would require far greater organization, resources, and planning.

The roots of the amphibious operations undertaken from 1861 through 1865 originated in a letter written by Major General Winfield Scott, Commander-in-Chief of the US Army, to President Abraham Lincoln on May 2, 1861. In this, Scott concluded that the rebellious states could only be defeated by "a cordon of posts on the Mississippi [River] to its mouth, from its junction with the Ohio, and by blockading ships of war on the sea-board" (Abraham Lincoln papers).

Although Lincoln had already ordered a blockade of the Confederacy on April 19, 1861, which was extended to include North Carolina and Virginia on April 27 after these states also seceded from the Union, he was much influenced by the popular cry of "On To Richmond" coined by Fitz Henry Warren, Washington correspondent of the *New York Daily Tribune*, who demanded a rapid advance overland to capture the newly created Confederate capital of Richmond, Virginia (*NYSWT*, April 26, 1861: 4.4). Others in Lincoln's cabinet, however, ignored the cries for quick military action, and derisory remarks about the "Anaconda Plan," and acted on Scott's advice.

On June 25, 1861, Secretary of the Navy Gideon Welles convened the Commission of Conference, more commonly called the Blockade Strategy Board. Chaired by Navy Captain Samuel F. Du Pont, it was composed of Alexander D. Bache of the US Coast Survey; Army Major John G. Barnard, a Corps of Engineers officer with extensive experience along the southern coast; and the Navy's Commander Charles H. Davis, who served as secretary but was actively involved in the work of the Board.

Of the seven reports the Blockade Strategy Board delivered to Welles between July 5 and September 19, 1861, that dated July 13 recommended the seizure and occupation of parts of the South Carolina coast to serve as "coaling stations and harbors of refuge for the blockading squadrons." Furthermore, it was suggested that the presence of large numbers of Union troops at such locations would prove "a sore annoyance to the rebels, and necessitate the constant maintenance of large forces" nearby, thus taking manpower away from the main Confederate army. The Board went on to recommend to Welles that a naval and military force "organized as an expedition and held in New York for a blow anywhere, would threaten ... the whole Southern coast" (*ORs*, I.53: 73).

Already under pressure from insurance underwriters due to the disruption to Northern shipping caused by Confederate privateers making forays out of Hatteras Inlet on the North Carolina coast, Welles directed that the focus of the operation should be switched from the coast of South Carolina to that of North Carolina, which would involve the capture of Forts Hatteras and Clark, on Hatteras Inlet, and probing farther inland to locations such as Roanoke Island and New Bern. These operations would

Established in June 1861, the Blockade Strategy Board consisted of Captain Samuel F. Du Pont, US Navy, who served as president; Alexander D. Bache, Superintendent of the US Coast Survey; Major John G. Barnard, US Army, Chief Engineer of the Department of Washington, DC; and Commander Charles H. Davis, US Navy, who served as secretary. The Board recommended the seizure and occupation of parts of the South Carolina coast to serve as "coaling stations and harbors of refuge for the blockading squadrons." (USNARA 111-B-3253/National Portrait Gallery, Smithsonian Institution S/NPG.77.47/USNARA 530217/USNARA 111-B-6194)

Photographed after his appointment as a rear admiral on February 7, 1863, John A. Dahlgren received the thanks of the US Congress in *Statutes at Large*, Vol. 12, "for distinguished service in the line of his profession, improvements in ordnance, and zealous and efficient labours in the ordnance branch of the service." (Library of Congress, LC-DIG-cwpbh-01195)

only involve the Navy facilitating Army landings, however. The development of Navy and other specialist units conducting amphibious actions came later in the Civil War and involved two prominent individuals.

During the antebellum years, naval officer John A. Dahlgren designed and developed a boat-howitzer capable of being carried on ship's launches, which was used by the US Navy. In 1863 he also created a Naval Brigade, which specialized in amphibious landings and land warfare once ashore. Canadian civilian engineer and inventor Norman K. Wiard developed a boat-howitzer similar to Dahlgren's and adopted by the US Army in 1862. He also designed and developed double-ended troop-carrying steamboats equipped with winches for speedily hoisting launches into the water. Furthermore, he encouraged the formation of the 1st New York Marine Artillery and Mississippi Marine Brigade, which penetrated the southern coastal estuaries and great rivers of the Mississippi Valley respectively.

Dahlgren began his naval career as a midshipman aboard the frigate *Macedonian* in 1826. Because of his mathematical proficiency and use of scientific instruments, Dahlgren was ordered to the US Coast Survey in April 1834, having received the rank of lieutenant. Assigned as Assistant Inspector of Ordnance at the Washington Navy Yard in 1847, he had within two years designed and introduced a smoothbore and rifled version of a 12-pounder boat-howitzer "complete in every detail, – lock, sight, and carriage; also the ammunition and equipment" (Dahlgren 1892: 133). These guns could be mounted on a carriage at the bow of a ship's launch and, when ashore, remounted within several minutes on a wrought-iron field carriage designed to be pulled into action by about 12 men using drag ropes.

Dahlgren's books *Form of Exercise and Manœuvre for the Boat-Howitzers of the U.S. Navy* and *System of Boat Armament in the United States Navy* were published in 1852. From 1856 through 1858, he commanded the Ordnance and Gunnery Practice sloop-of-war *Plymouth* during which time the crew was drilled in the use of his boat-howitzers, his 9in shell guns, and "Plymouth" rifle muskets. Returning to duty in Washington in 1859 as Chief of the Bureau of Ordnance with the rank of commander, he was appointed Commandant of the Washington Navy Yard on April 22, 1861, following the resignation of Captain Franklin Buchanan, who joined the Confederate Navy.

Born in 1825, Norman Wiard was from a family of metalworkers and blacksmiths. As an iron foundry foreman, he developed a lifelong proclivity for inventing new technologies. At the age of 25 he was part owner of N. Wiard & Co., fabricators of machinery, and in 1852 he became foreman of the Moses Steam Engine Works in Chicago, Illinois (*CWT*, March 1, 1856: 3.3). Moving to Janesville, Wisconsin, in 1856 he became Superintendent of the Western Novelty Works, which produced "Stationery, Portable and Marine Steam Engines" (*SPWM*, July 26, 1856: 3.5). In 1859 he began the design and construction of a steam-powered "ice boat" called *Lady Franklin* that was capable of skating along the frozen surface of rivers, but it failed its trials during early 1861 (*DDN*, January 11, 1861: 2.3).

With the outbreak of the Civil War, Wiard established workshops in New York City to make steel rifled artillery pieces for Union Army and Navy service, including boat-howitzers based on the design of those developed by Dahlgren. Having a dim view of Dahlgren's iron-barreled boat-howitzers, Wiard developed a similar 12-pounder and 6-pounder weapon with a rifled, semi-steel barrel composed of a mixture of low-carbon cast iron and scrap steel. This meant his guns were less likely to explode than those invented by Dahlgren, which had either bronze or iron barrels. Each of Wiard's guns was provided with the same type of carriage and implements for use on land or at sea as those of Dahlgren. Wiard promoted the use of his steamboats, guns and launches with sliding and field carriages in *Marine Artillery as Adapted for Service on the Coast and on Inland Waters*, published in 1863.

Although Wiard failed to sell his ideas to the Navy, Army commander Brigadier General Ambrose E. Burnside recognized their merits and ordered his boat-howitzers and launches for his expedition on the North Carolina coast in 1862. Likewise, Wiard's steamboat winch system was adapted for use inland by the Mississippi Marine Brigade.

Posing in front of a row of his 6-pounder rifled boat-howitzers and carriages at the Washington Navy Yard, this civilian has been identified as the inventor and ordnance manufacturer Norman K. Wiard, who was appointed as Superintendent of Ordnance Stores for the Burnside Expedition in 1862. (Library of Congress LOC pnp-cwpb-03600-03649)

HATTERAS INLET, AUGUST 28–29, 1861

Soon after Secretary of the Navy Welles received the July 13 report of the Blockade Strategy Board, he began to implement its recommendations. Initially he sought to block the channels leading out of Hatteras Inlet by sinking old hulks, or blockships, in their path, and ordered Navy Commander Henry S. Stellwagen to go to Chesapeake Bay to purchase such vessels. At the same time, Stellwagen was ordered to report his activities to Flag Officer Silas H. Stringham, commandant of the Atlantic Blockading Squadron. Stringham opposed the plan to block the inlets, however, believing that the tidal currents would either sweep the impediments away or rapidly scour new channels. Thus, he concluded that an effective blockade of that part of the North Carolina coast could only be achieved if the inlets were in Union hands, which would involve the capture of Forts Hatteras and Clark. As the Navy could not undertake such an operation alone, the cooperation of the Army was necessary.

Although the Army needed to secure operational bases and seize key locations on land in Virginia and along the Mississippi River and its tributaries, its commanders acknowledged the role it would have to play in strangling the Confederacy via operations along the southern coastline. As a result, Major General Benjamin F. Butler was ordered to assemble a force of 860 men for the expedition (*ORs*, I.4: 580). He selected 500 from the predominantly German-speaking 20th New York Infantry, Colonel Max Weber commanding; 220 (Cos C, G, and H) from the 9th New York Infantry, also known as Hawkins' Zouaves, Colonel Rush C. Hawkins commanding; and 100 from the 99th New York Infantry, or Union Coast Guard, Captain Richard Nixon, Co. A, commanding. This force would be spearheaded by Marines from the Navy warships involved in the operation, plus 60 Army regulars from Co. B, 2d US Artillery, under Captain Frank H. Larned. The volunteer troops were placed aboard the steamers *Adelaide* and *George Peabody*, two of the vessels that Stellwagen had chartered for Government service.

Adelaide was described as "a staunch side-wheel steamer, capable of making sixteen miles [over 13 knots] per hour, and a first rate sea boat" (*ES*, August 14, 1861: 2.1). Stellwagen would command *Adelaide* during the expedition. *George Peabody* was of 1,000 tons burthen, and was placed under Lieutenant Reigart B. Lowry. Both vessels were fitted with masts in case their engines failed, and armed with four 32-pounder guns located fore and aft. Temporarily under the command of Navy officers, their crews were protected by an armed guard.

While Butler gathered his landing force, Stringham learned that War Department orders to Major General John E. Wool, Butler's superior, stipulated that as the expedition originated in the Navy Department it should remain under Navy control. As a result, Stringham devised his own plan of attack and gathered his naval force off Fortress Monroe at Hampton Roads, Virginia. His plan was to use dismasted schooners and surfboats as landing craft. These were to be packed with troops and towed by shallow-draught tugboats close to the shoreline. When released the surfboats were to be steered or rowed on to the beach by sailors while Navy gunboats provided covering fire.

The seven warships Stringham chose for the expedition were the screw frigate *Minnesota* as his flagship, commanded by Captain Gershom J. Van Brunt, with Butler and his aides aboard; the sailing sloop-of-war *Cumberland*, Captain John Marston; the side-wheel frigate *Susquehanna*,

Captain John S. Chauncey; the steam frigate *Wabash*, Captain Samuel Mercer; the steam sloop *Pawnee*, Commander Stephen C. Rowan, which transported Co. B, 2d Artillery; the gunboat *Monticello*, Commander John P. Gillis; and the side-wheel steamer *Harriet Lane*, Commander John Faunce. All but the last vessel were ships of the US Navy – *Harriet Lane* served in the US Revenue Cutter Service. Also included were the armed steam tugboats *Fanny*, commanded by Lieutenant Peirce Crosby, and *Adriatic*, Captain Thompson, plus the sailing vessels *Alvarado*, *Ellen Goldsboro*, and *Mary and Hetty*, under the charge of First Lieutenant James Millward, Jr., Co. F, 99th New York Infantry.

The larger landing boats to be used were placed in charge of Master John S. Barnes, of *Wabash*, on August 26, 1861 who was sent into Hampton Bay with two cutters to dismast and dismantle two schooners, tie them alongside two larger steamboats and, with a small tugboat, tow them alongside *Minnesota* (Hayes 1962: 74). These cutters were supplemented by numerous large surfboats designed for beach landing and hastily constructed for the Navy under the direction of government agents in several seaboard cities. For example, a correspondent for the *Brooklyn Daily Eagle* reported seeing "a large number of hands … constantly employed in turning out surf boats … at Ingersoll's Boat Bazaar on South Street, New York," in August 1861 (*BDE*, August 27, 1861: 3.1).

Departing Chesapeake Bay about 1600hrs on August 26, 1861, the small squadron became separated as *Minnesota* and *Wabash* fell behind the faster *Monticello* and the steamers *Adelaide* and *George Peabody*. As a result, it was not until 1630hrs the next day that most of the vessels needed for the operation were assembled off Hatteras Inlet. This caused much complaint on the transports, according to a correspondent of the *New York Daily Tribune* aboard *Adelaide*, because many believed the landing could have been completed on the day of arrival and while the weather was good. Of that evening, the *New York Daily Tribune* correspondent wrote:

> The Commodore's flag has been hauled down … The fine band on the deck of the Minnesota is playing patriotic airs … The tall masts of the matchless frigates stand out against the sky, now glowing with the last rays of set sun. The Commodore's boat goes from ship to ship, delivering orders for the morrow. Sentinels are posted on deck and in cabin, and the disappointment … gives place to buoyant hope. (*NYDT*, September 3, 1861: 6.1)

According to the official report of Flag Officer Stringham, the morning of August 28, 1861, brought southerly winds and "heavy surf rolling on the beach," which did not bode well for the landings (*ORNs*, I.6: 121). At 0820hrs, *Wabash*, with *Cumberland* in tow, steamed in toward Fort Clark, which was the smaller of the two Confederate forts at Hatteras Inlet. *Minnesota* followed them, plus *Susquehanna*, which arrived off Hatteras Inlet late having just completed a seven-week overhaul at Philadelphia. The bombardment of Fort Clark began at 1000hrs.

Appointed Flag Officer of the Atlantic Blockading Squadron in 1861, Silas H. Stringham entered the US Navy in 1809 and saw active service during the War of 1812 (1812–15), the Second Barbary War (1815), and the Mexican–American War (1846–48). His tactic of firing from a moving vessel reversed the advantages previously held by land-based artillery against relatively stationary warships. (Author's collection)

Benjamin F. Butler was the first major general to be appointed by President Abraham Lincoln into the new Union Army of volunteers. A powerful politician from Massachusetts, Butler had no background in military matters other than some militia participation. His lack of military experience would prove costly to the Union. (Author's collection)

Charles Norton enlisted for three months in Co. H (Mechanic Rifles Co. No. 2), 1st Rhode Island Detached Militia, on April 12, 1861. He fought at First Bull Run, or First Manassas, on July 21, 1861, and was mustered-out on August 2, 1861. He then enlisted for three years in the Union Navy at New Bedford, Massachusetts, on August 7, 1861, and several weeks later witnessed the amphibious landing at Hatteras Inlet from the deck of the steam sloop *Pawnee*. (Author's collection)

A first at Hatteras Inlet was Stringham's employment of his steam-powered vessels in an elliptical pattern, constantly moving and firing against fixed artillery. This tactic reversed the success rate previously held by land-based artillery competing against relatively stationary warships. Steam-powered vessels could be maneuvered without concern for wind and tides, which gave them a distinct tactical superiority.

In a letter to his brother Timothy, Private Daniel O'Connor, one of 16 Marines remaining aboard *Cumberland* and first loader on the starboard after gun, wrote:

> the Wabash comminced hostilliys by 1 of her buldogs barking the downfall of Jefferson Davis ... bang bang was the order of the day for 1 hour & ½ we fired as hard as we could throwing shel in to the enemys battery like showers of hail & knocked down their flag staff ... the Suskahanna came in during the firing which added 1 more to our number ... we spliced the main brace & drank Uncle Sams health ... during the firing none of the ships came to anchor ... they went round & round trough and fro so as the rebles could not get our range ... we had 2 after guns in the cabin ... one port & 1 stabord ... the smoke bothered us a good deal but ... we made some splinded shots. (Daniel O'Connor Letters, September 18, 1861)

Meanwhile *Pawnee*, *Monticello*, *Harriet Lane*, and the transport vessels had reached the site of a wrecked ship about 2 miles northeast of Fort Clark. The troops involved had been woken at 0400hrs and given "an early breakfast" (*ORNs*, I.6: 121). The plan as devised by Major General Butler was to land approximately 1,000 troops who would launch a flank attack on the Confederate forts approximately 2 miles farther down the coast. When landed the order of advance would consist of the 9th New York Infantry on the right, the 20th New York Infantry on the left, and the Army Regulars and 99th New York Infantry detachment in the center, with the artillery manned by sailors and supported by Marines.

Proposing to join the landings, Butler was transferred to *Harriet Lane* in order to direct operations, along with 37 Marines of *Minnesota* detailed to

Published in *Harper's Weekly* on September 14, 1861, this engraving shows the bombardment of Forts Hatteras and Clark by the warships commanded by Flag Officer Silas H. Stringham in preparation for the amphibious landing at Hatteras Inlet on August 28, 1861. (Author's collection)

go ashore, commanded by Captain William J. Shuttleworth. Making up the rest of the Marine detachment assigned for landing were 44 Marines from *Wabash* under Captain Isaac T. Doughty, and 27 Marines from *Cumberland* under First Lieutenant Charles Heywood. To provide firepower once the men were ashore, two Dahlgren 12-pounder boat-howitzers, one rifled and the other smoothbore, loaned by the Navy, were hoisted from *Minnesota* into one of the surfboats, which was sent across to *Adelaide* from which troops scrambled down into it.

Harriet Lane cruised around the other vessels to cheers. At this point the *New York Daily Tribune* correspondent noted: "The weather begins to thicken up, and the wind freshens. The delay consequent on the distribution of forces among the ships and the placing of guns in small boats to be used in landing is vexatious in the extreme" (*NYDT*, September 3, 1861: 6.2).

At 1130hrs the guns of *Pawnee*, *Monticello*, and *Harriet Lane* opened fire on the beach and the landing operation began. Forming the first assault wave, the Marines were transferred from *Harriet Lane* into the shallow-draught tugboats *Fanny* and *Adriatic*, which took them closer to the shore. The Marines climbed down into the large surfboats and sailors rowed them to the beach. Owing to strong winds, only 54 Marines plus several officers struggled ashore through the breaking waves and crashing surf. Their boats ran aground on the beach and the sailors found it impossible to get them back into the water to collect more of the intended landing party.

Other troops were loaded into the two dismasted schooners, towed near the wreck and anchored, and the men were then transferred into surfboats. These entered the surf and narrowly escaped capsizing as they were thrown up onto the beach with the sea rolling in torrents over their sterns. The troops jumped into waist-deep water and waded ashore.

Elements of the 20th, 99th, and 9th New York Infantry went ashore next. Packed into the schooners, they were towed close into the shore by the transports *Adelaide* and *George Peabody*, and then transferred into surfboats that were soon engulfed by the surf but also avoided capsizing. According to Colonel Max Weber, who landed with the 20th New York Infantry: "All of us were wet up to the shoulders, cut off entirely from the fleet, with wet ammunition, and without provisions" (*ORs*, I.4: 589).

A cutter from *Pawnee* landed safely and, returning to one of the schooners, took more men on board, but on entering the surf again was swamped and the troops barely escaped drowning as they struggled ashore.

The last troops to attempt to land included the 9th New York Infantry. In the regimental history, Sergeant Matthew J. Graham, Co. A, recorded that the troops were "transferred to small boats, and long strings of these, one behind the other, like great strings of beads, were towed by small steamers" (Graham 1900: 122) to within a short distance of the shore before being rowed in through the huge breaking waves. Of the landing, Corporal John H.E. Whitney, Co. B, wrote:

> It was a dangerous feat to perform – spring[ing] out of the boats and wading through the heavy, rolling surf. There was great fear that many lives would be lost; but they all assisted one another, and after considerable, almost superhuman effort, they succeeded in getting safely on the land. A few of the other troops were landed in the same manner, when it was declared impossible to debark any more. (Whitney 1866: 52–53)

Private Daniel O'Connor was part of the Marine detachment aboard the sloop-of-war *Cumberland*, which took part in the bombardment of Fort Clark, Hatteras Inlet, on August 28, 1861. O'Connor served throughout the Civil War, surviving the ramming and sinking of *Cumberland* by the ironclad CSS *Virginia* in Hampton Roads on March 8, 1862. (Author's collection)

Sergeant Graham concluded: "The Ninth being among the last regiments to reach the shore, found the ground over which the other troops had passed much cut up and actually knee deep with mud. The short distance they marched from landing to bivouac was literally waded" (Graham 1900: 122).

By this time the fierce wind and breaking waves made further landing attempts impossible. In his after-action report, Major General Butler stated: "I was on board the Harriet Lane, directing the disembarkation of the troops by means of signals, and was about landing with them at the time the boats were stove. We were induced to desist from further attempts at landing troops by the rising of the wind" (*ORs*, I.4: 582).

Once ashore, Colonel Weber, as the senior officer present, organized the diminished and demoralized landing force by having the men formed in line and counted. He established that he had present: 45 men of Co. B, 2d US Artillery, commanded by First Lieutenant Larned; 45 Marines under Captain Shuttleworth; 70 men of Co. G, 9th New York Infantry, under Captain Edward Jardine; 102 men of Cos H and K of his own regiment; 28 men of the 99th New York Infantry under Captain Nixon; and 28 sailors under Lieutenant Crosby, which included those assigned to crew the Dahlgren boat-howitzers, making a total of only 318 officers and men of the 880 taking part in the landing operation. He next posted pickets under the command of Larned, while the bulk of Weber's force waited for several hours in hopes that more men could be landed.

Meanwhile, several boats carrying troops drifted about on the water. Having lost their oars in the attempt to pass through the surf, they helplessly rode the waves, waiting to be rescued. Boat crews from *Susquehanna* eventually picked up 40 Marines and 60 soldiers from the 20th New York Infantry. Their wretched condition when taken aboard gave rise to much concern for their comrades ashore.

At 1350hrs the fleet ceased firing having observed the Confederate garrison retreating from Fork Clark toward Fort Hatteras in its rear.

A **HAWKINS' ZOUAVES AT HATTERAS INLET, AUGUST 28, 1861**

Elements of the 9th New York Infantry, also known as Hawkins' Zouaves, land via surfboats on Hatteras Inlet, North Carolina, on August 28, 1861. The first major amphibious landing of the Civil War was disrupted by gale-force winds and high surf that stove many of the boats and caused the landings to be called off, leaving 323 troops stranded on the beach overnight. Re-forming at the point where they had struggled ashore, these men spent a miserable night ashore in a driving rain. Although vulnerable to attack from the Confederate garrison at Forts Hatteras and Clark, Colonel William F. Martin, commanding the Confederate defences in the forts, overestimated their numbers and lost the initiative, surrendering to Flag Officer Silas H. Stringham, USN, the next day.

Observing this, Weber sent 20 men under Lieutenant Colonel Francis Weiss, accompanied by volunteer aide and ordnance officer Second Lieutenant William H. Weigel, to reconnoiter the situation at Fort Clark, which was about 2 miles from the landing point. Reinforced by Cos H and K of the 20th New York Infantry led by Weber, the fort was occupied by the Union force with Weiss capturing a secession flag still flying from the breastworks, and a small "Stars and Stripes" flag being raised by Captain Walter Johnson of the 99th New York Infantry. Under the impression that the Confederates had returned to their posts, the guns aboard the Union ships recommenced firing, which drove Weber and his men out of the earthworks and back along the beach with one man slightly wounded.

Under the mistaken belief that both forts had now been abandoned, Stringham next ordered *Monticello* closer in shore to take possession of the works, but that vessel immediately came under fire from the guns of Fort Hatteras and the general action was renewed. The bombardment continued until 1815hrs when threatening weather conditions convinced Stringham to cease fire for the day and withdraw his vessels to the safety of deeper waters.

Meanwhile, the stranded landing party re-formed on the beach at the spot where they had scrambled ashore, and spent a miserable night in the rain. Overestimating their numbers, Colonel William F. Martin, commander of the Confederate defenses in the forts, failed to attack them believing the Union numbers were greater than they actually were. At 0800hrs the next morning the squadron opened fire on Fort Hatteras and after three hours of further bombardment the Confederate flag was lowered, and its garrison of 615 men surrendered.

The capture of Forts Hatteras and Clark represented the first amphibious operation and first significant Union victory of the Civil War. It did much to encourage Union supporters following the embarrassment of defeat at First Bull Run, or First Manassas, on July 21, 1861. Stringham's new tactic of keeping his steamers in motion while bombarding the forts did much to eliminate the traditional advantage of shore-based guns over those carried aboard ships. It was also the first large-scale combined operation of the Civil War involving both the Union Army and Navy. At the same time, the Navy wished to divest itself of the responsibility of moving the Army's men, supplies, and equipment by sea. Writing to Assistant Secretary of the Navy Gustavus V. Fox on September 13, 1861, Stringham pointed out that the responsibility for the provision of transports and surfboats "more properly" belonged to the Army (*ORNs*, I.6: 205). This resulted in the development and expansion of the Union Army's own fleet throughout the remainder of the Civil War.

Based on a sketch by Alfred R. Waud, and published in the *New York Illustrated News* on September 14, 1861, this engraving depicts Colonel Max Weber forming the troops into ranks and counting them to ascertain the size of the force successfully landed. (Author's collection)

ROANOKE ISLAND, FEBRUARY 7–8, 1862

About a month after the capture of Hatteras Island, Colonel Rush Hawkins was on leave in Washington, DC, and was invited to the White House to confer with President Lincoln and General-in-Chief George B. McClellan about the possibility of further combined operations against Pamlico Sound, North Carolina (Symonds 2010: 12). The idea became the objective of the North Carolina Expedition commanded by Brigadier General Burnside, who was tasked with the creation of an Army Coast Division, which he considered should be composed of fishermen, dockworkers, and others with maritime experience from the Northeastern states. Burnside's reasoning was that such men would already be familiar with the handling of large and small vessels and therefore easier to train.

These engravings of Brigadier General Ambrose E. Burnside (above) and Flag Officer Louis M. Goldsborough, who separately commanded the Army and Navy operations during the amphibious landings on Roanoke Island, were published in *Harper's Weekly* on March 1, 1862. (Author's collection)

Initially Burnside intended to base his operations in Chesapeake Bay, but this was soon changed to an assault on the interior coast of North Carolina, beginning with the capture of Roanoke Island. The change of plan was based on a belief in the War Department that pro-Union sentiment was being suppressed in North Carolina, and an invasion would allow Union supporters to express their true loyalties (Browning 1993: 19–21). On January 7, 1862, McClellan issued General Order No. 2, which stated that North Carolina should thereafter constitute a separate military command known as the Department of North Carolina (*ORs*, I.9: 353). Six days later Burnside assumed command of the new Department, and the invasion of North Carolina came to be known as the Burnside Expedition.

As recruiting for the expedition progressed, Burnside gathered the Coast Division in camp at Annapolis, Maryland, and organized it into three brigades led by friends from his United States Military Academy days. Brigadier General John G. Foster commanded the 1st Brigade; Brigadier General Jesse L. Reno, the 2d Brigade; and Brigadier General John G. Parke, the 3d Brigade. Also attached to the Coast Division were unassigned troops consisting of a detachment of the 1st New York Marine Artillery, led by Colonel William A. Howard, and Co. B, 99th New York Infantry under Lieutenant Colonel Charles W. Tillotson.

Appointed as Superintendent of Ordnance Stores for the expedition, the inventor and ordnance manufacturer Norman Wiard was directed to consult with Howard, and supply his unit with guns, carriages, and implements. Accordingly, Wiard provided 12 steel 12-pounder and four steel 6-pounder rifled boat-howitzers, each with a sliding boat and field carriage. These guns were carried aboard Burnside's Army gunboats but were not used during the land operation on Roanoke Island as the Navy preferred to use the boat-howitzers developed by John Dahlgren.

By January 31, 1862, 12,829 officers and men were assigned to the Coast Division and ready for duty (*ORs*, I.9: 358). While the Union Navy flotilla, under Flag Officer Louis M. Goldsborough, would provide most of the heavy firepower during the proposed landings, Burnside sought to acquire gunboats to be under Army control, and this immediately led to rivalry between the two branches of service. The Navy had few oceangoing vessels with shallow enough draught to pass through Hatteras Inlet into the waters surrounding Roanoke Island, and therefore had to purchase merchant vessels suitable for conversion. At the same time, Burnside's agents were seeking similar vessels. As the experienced seafarers of the Navy were able to acquire the most suitable ships, the Army was left with those that were barely seaworthy.

By the time the Army part of the expedition got underway from Annapolis to rendezvous with the Navy at Fortress Monroe on January 9, 1862, it consisted of nine armed troop-carrying gunboats; 12 troop-carrying sailing vessels, five of which were armed with one gun; five horse-carrying schooners; five supply schooners; two schooners carrying pontoon bridges; one siege train schooner, and one hospital ship (*PI*, January 18, 1862: 2.4 & 5). The whole Army fleet was commanded by Lieutenant Ernest Staples, USN. Each vessel in Burnside's Army fleet was designated by a signal number, and the vessels in each brigade were known by a different colored flag. The 1st Brigade was designated by a red flag with white numbers, the 2d Brigade by a blue flag with white numbers, and the 3d Brigade by a red-and-blue flag with white numbers (*CT*, January 15, 1862: 1.3).

On arrival at Hampton Roads, the Union fleet was joined by 20 Navy gunboats and five floating batteries. With troop transports and other ancillary vessels, the whole armada consisted of 60 ships of all classes. It was not until setting sail two days later that the captain of each ship opened sealed orders and learned that his vessel should proceed to the vicinity of Cape Hatteras and attack Roanoke Island.

The planned assault, albeit under divided command, called for Navy gunboats to clear the enemy from the landing place while transports approached to within approximately 3 miles from the shoreline. There the troops would be loaded into two lines of about 20 surfboats temporarily linked together by hawsers and towed by two small shallow-draught steamers. Approaching the beach at speed, the steamers would cast off the surfboats and veer away while still at a safe distance from the beach. The surfboats in turn then would cast off the connecting hawsers, and with their acquired velocity independently glide through the water and up on to the beach with the help of a steersman. Six launches carrying five Dahlgren boat-howitzers and one smoothbore gun, and commanded by a Navy midshipman, would also be rowed ashore to cover the troops while in shallow water or on land. Once the whole Coast Division was ashore, the plan was to advance north along Roanoke Island next morning and capture the main Confederate redoubts, thus getting in the rear of all the shore batteries to seize and silence them.

The voyage south was the worst part of the Burnside Expedition for the Union troops. Burnside earned the admiration and respect of his command by swapping his comfortable quarters, and that of his staff, aboard the transport *George Peabody*, for the Army gunboat *Picket*. When two days of violent storms struck while the armada was on its way south and off Cape Hatteras, four vessels were lost, although all persons aboard were rescued. The four vessels were the screw steamer *City of New York*, laden with ordnance and supplies; the side-wheel steamer *Pocahontas*, carrying horses; the Army gunboat *Zouave*; and the floating battery *Grapeshot*. Three troop transports, consisting of the steamers *Eastern Queen* and *Louisiana*, and the bark *Voltigeur*, were grounded, and four men including Colonel Joseph W. Allen, commanding the 9th New Jersey Infantry, were drowned endeavoring to reach the shore in a surfboat.

The narrow passage into Pamlico Sound, about 2 miles off the southern end of Roanoke Island, through Hatteras Inlet was time consuming. After passing over the "Snarl," or sand bars, vessels found that the "Swash," or passage into Pamlico Sound, thought to be 8ft deep, was only 6ft. The

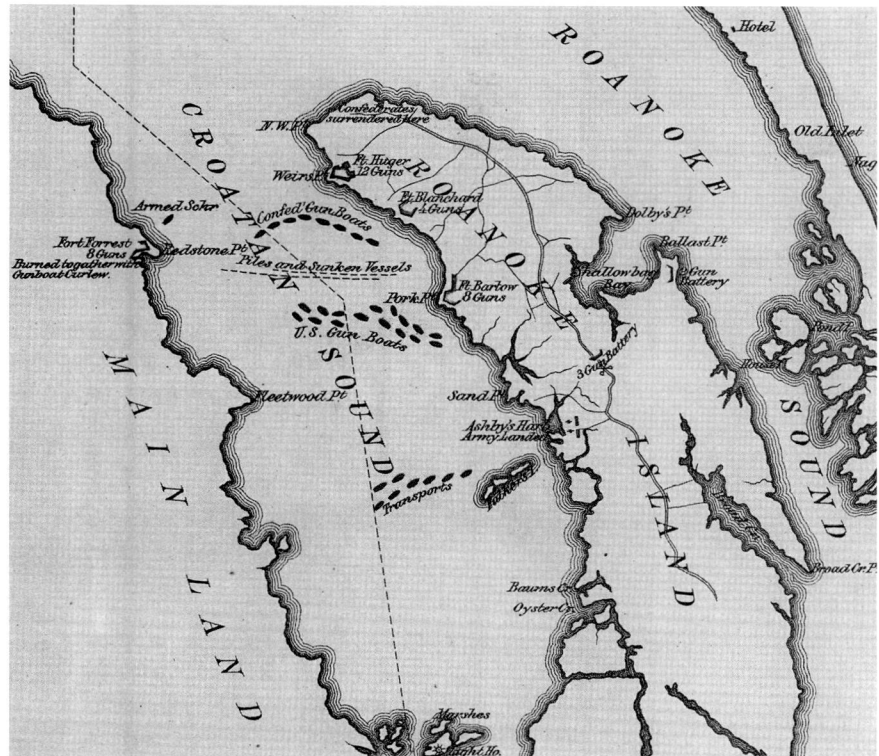

This map attributed to Second Lieutenant William S. Andrews, 9th New York Infantry, shows the deployment of Union Army and Navy gunboats, and opposing Confederate Army gunboats, during the amphibious landings on Roanoke Island on February 7, 1862. (Library of Congress)

draught of some Army gunboats was too deep to get across, and they had to be lightened and hauled through Hatteras Inlet using a hawser attached at a distance to an anchor, known as kedging. Where other vessels were too deep to be kedged in, the troops and materials aboard were brought ashore on Hatteras Island, and the vessels sent back north.

It was not until nightfall on February 5 that most vessels were anchored in Pamlico Sound. Despite rain and fog the next day, the fleet moved closer to the narrow channel leading into Croatan Sound. On February 7 the weather improved, and Navy gunboats steamed north and divided with some ordered to fire on Fort Bartow on Pork Point, while others concentrated their fire on the seven vessels of the Confederate Mosquito Fleet to their north commanded by Commodore William F. Lynch.

The naval bombardment began at 1130hrs and revealed the weakness of the Confederate defenses. Only four of the nine guns at Fort Bartow, situated on the west side of Roanoke Island, could bear on the Union gunboats. Those at Forts Huger and Blanchard were out of range and could not contribute at all. On the North Carolina mainland, Fort Forrest, a set of anchored barges equipped with seven guns, attempted to reach the Union gunboats as they came within range. Onboard the Army troop transport *Zouave*, a member of the 25th Massachusetts Infantry recalled: "It was quite an interesting and exciting sight to see the gun-boats pass one by one through the narrow channel, and gradually draw near the island. The attack was commenced about half past eleven, and continued brisk and steady during the day, our boats firing about five shots to their two" (*BR*, March 13, 1862, 42:4).

Commanding the Navy side-wheel gunboat *Hunchback*, Acting Lieutenant Edmund R. Colhoun recalled:

We steadily advancing, and pouring such a hail of shot and shell among their gun-boats, that they commenced retreating to get out of the way. About the same time their battery opened on us. One of our one hundred pounder rifled shot struck the rebel steamer "Curlew" about amidship, and went right through her; she immediately hauled off, and they had to run her ashore under a battery on the main land to prevent her sinking ... The rebel gun-boats having retreated so far that our shot could barely reach them, the Commodore made signal to close in with the battery; so the old "Hunchback" headed in that way. Steadily we advanced though slowly, as we were shoaling our water. I went in as far as my draught would permit, say about 1,400 yards from it, and let them have it from my nine inch guns and one hundred pounder at 3.30 p.m. One of their shot struck my engine and disabled it. I dropped anchor and sprung my broadside to the battery, where I remained during the action, which lasted until dark. When the rebel gunboats saw our main efforts were directed towards the battery, they came down close enough to reach us with their rifled guns, and I was thus a good part of the time exposed to their cross fire. Though we were in the thickest of the engagement, and were struck eight times, yet a merciful Providence watched over us and nobody was hurt ... One shot went through my cabin, covering the deck with splinters; one through the hull just above the waterline, (a thirty-two pound shot, which we have on board,) and one through our smoke pipe ... while all this was going on, our army was landing about half a mile below the battery. (*LO*, March 7, 1862: 2.6)

As Burnside's troop transports arrived off the intended landing place at Ashby's Harbor, the Army gunboat *Picket* and Navy gunboat *Delaware* were ordered into the mouth of the harbor to cover the landings. They fired a few shells inland, and with no return fire Burnside concluded that the defenders lacked gun batteries in that vicinity. At 1300hrs he ordered a small surfboat with 20-year-old Second Lieutenant William S. Andrews, of Co. K, 9th New York Infantry, and six enlisted men of the Rhode Island Battalion, into Ashby's Harbor to take soundings and examine the landing area. Having successfully completed their mission, Andrews and his party were fired on by Confederate sharpshooters as they rowed back out to the fleet, wounding a Rhode Islander in the jaw.

Having received Andrews' report by 1500hrs, Burnside ordered the landings to begin, and at 1600hrs the troops began reaching the shore.

Entitled "The Burnside Expedition – Landing of the national troops on Roanoke Island, under cover of the Union gunboats Delaware and Picket," this engraving was published in *Frank Leslie's Illustrated Newspaper* on March 8, 1862 (p.245), and depicts three surfboats crammed with troops plus boat-howitzers linked together by hawsers being towed by a tugboat toward the beach. Other surfboats carrying troops are being rowed ashore by Union Navy sailors. (Author's collection)

Published in *Frank Leslie's Illustrated Newspaper* on April 27, 1861, this engraving depicts sailors sponging out a Dahlgren 12-pounder boat-howitzer during a landing exercise ashore. (Naval History and Heritage Command NH 73724)

A 200-strong Confederate force led by Colonel John V. Jordan, commanding the 31st North Carolina Infantry, posted in the woods to oppose the landing, was discovered and fired on by the gunboats. The defenders fled without any attempt to return fire and there was no further opposition. Almost all of the 10,000 men of the Coast Division present were ashore by midnight.

In his after-battle report, Burnside described the landings in the following detail:

> In less than twenty minutes from the time the boats reached the shore 4,000 of our men were passing over the marshes at a double-quick and forming in most perfect order on the dry land near the house; and I beg leave to say that I never witnessed a more beautiful sight than that presented by the approach of these vessels to the shore and the landing and forming of the troops. Each brigadier-general had a light-draught steamer, to which were attached some 20 surf-boats in a long line in the rear. Both steamers and boats were densely filled with soldiers, and each boat bearing the national flag. As the steamers approached the shore at a rapid speed each surf-boat was "let go," and with their acquired velocity and direction of the steersman reached the shore in line. (*ORs*, I.9: 76)

In a letter home dated February 10, 1862, Captain Benjamin S. Pardue, commanding Co. A, 10th Connecticut Infantry, wrote:

> the signal was given us to land. We loaded, got into our boats, and pulled for the pilot buoy, and then in two long lines were towed to shore some three miles distant. In the woods we could see the glitter of hundreds of bayonets; but still on we steadily went, cheering. A gunboat [the armed schooner *Delaware*] came up and sent a shell howling like a fiend through the woods. The bayonet glimmer departed. Ashore, the first American flag was carried by a Massachusetts regiment, but the proud motto of old Connecticut, "Qui Trans[tulit] Sust[inet],"

Produced by William Momberger, a German-American immigrant and prolific landscape painter and illustrator in the mid-19th century, this colored engraving depicts the unchallenged landing of the troops of Brigadier General John G. Foster's 1st Brigade on Roanoke Island, North Carolina, on February 7, 1862. Note the boat-howitzer being pulled ashore in the distance. (Author's collection)

[He Who Transplanted Still Sustains] was next to follow. (*NLDC*, February 25, 1862: 2.2)

Also writing home, an unidentified member of Co. H of the same regiment stated: "We landed without firing muskets. Capt. [Robert] Leggett was the first man ashore and ours was the first company ashore. We went into the woods as soon as possible, and the way we slashed through mud and water up to our knees was a caution" (*NLDC*, February 27, 1862: 2.3).

A member of the 5th Rhode Island Infantry recalled: "By half-past ten that evening, all the forces had landed, waded through a swamp knee-deep with mud, and gathered around their camp-fires. Here was to be our resting place until morning" (*EP*, February 22, 1862: 2.3).

Meanwhile, commanding the six launches, Midshipman Benjamin H. Porter and his gun crews, consisting mainly of Army personnel, dragged their five boat-howitzers and one smoothbore through a swamp to dry ground. Marching inland to the road beyond the beach, they set up their guns to protect the troops as they bivouacked. There they stood guard all night, drenched by persistent rain.

At daylight on February 8, the 25th Massachusetts Infantry of Foster's 1st Brigade supported by Porter's guns was ordered to advance north along

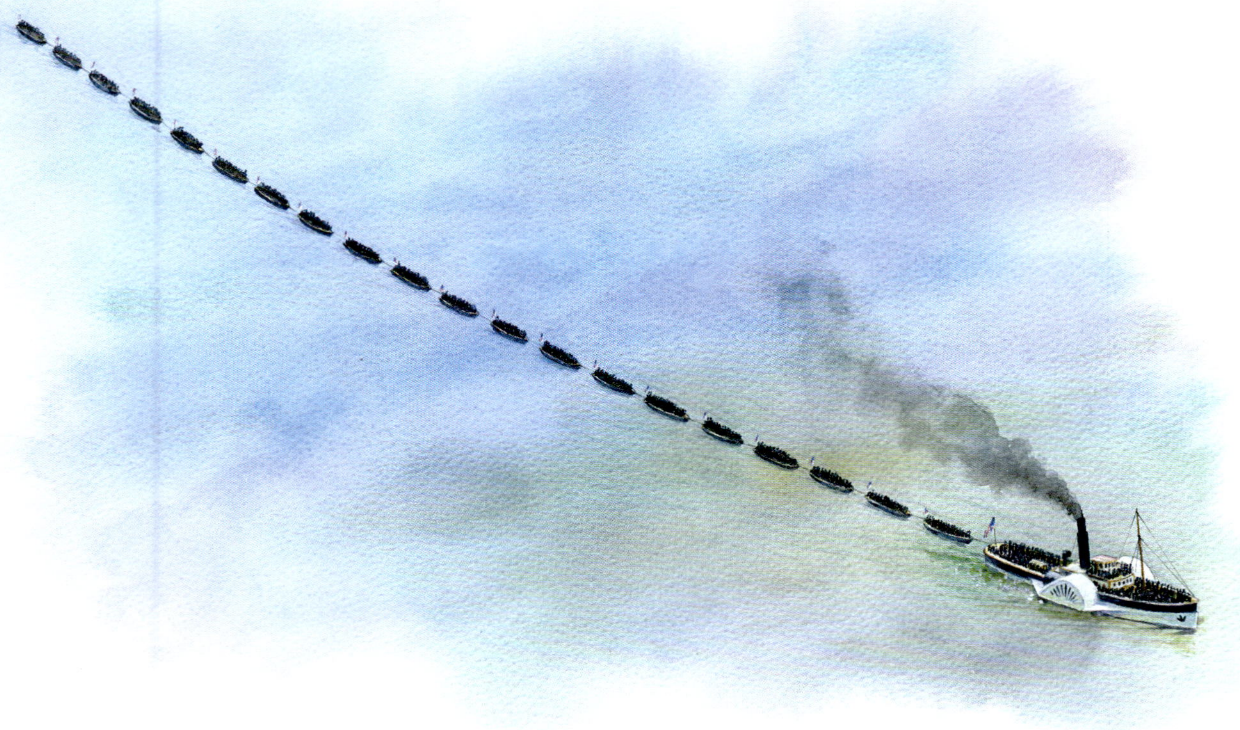

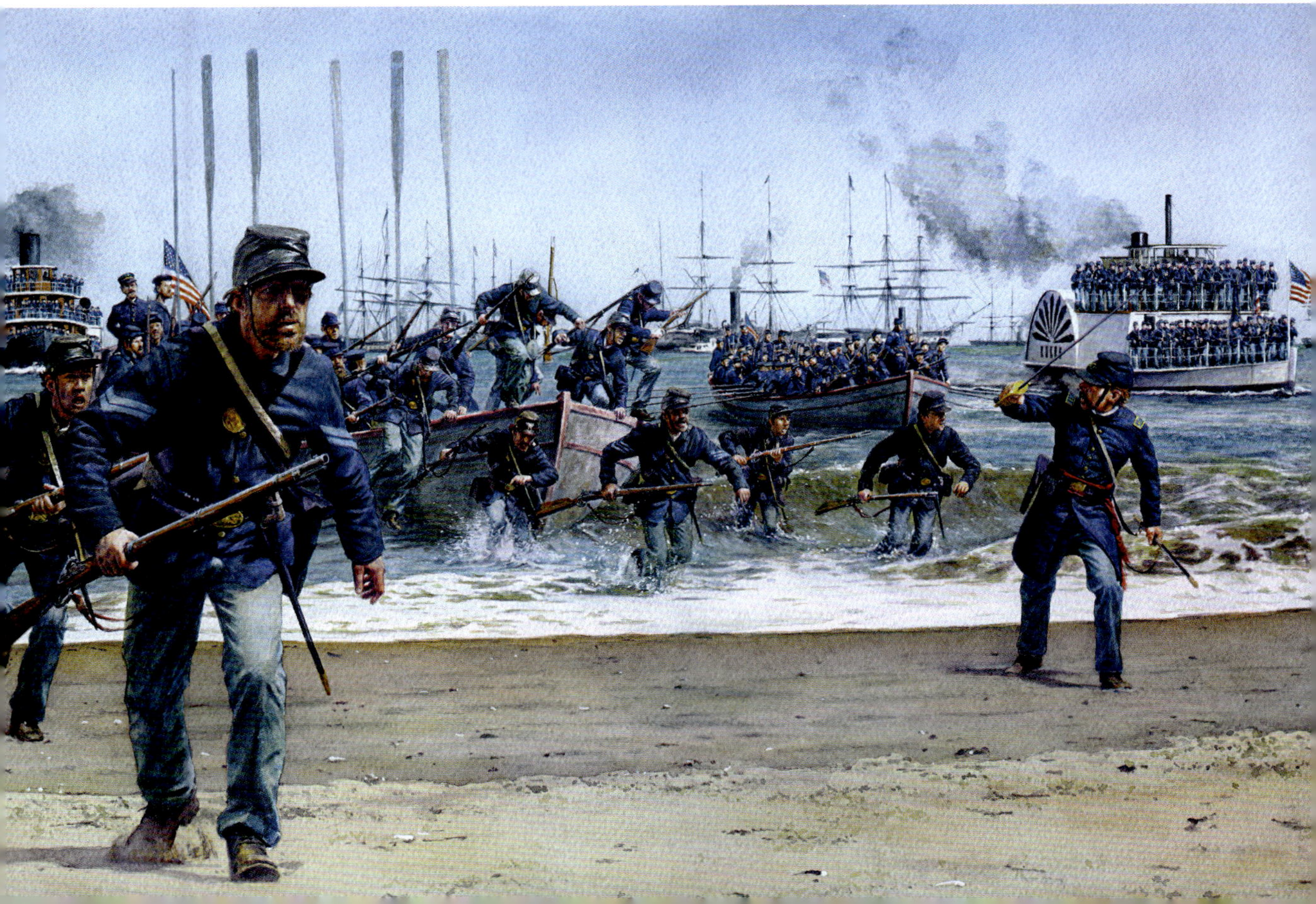

a narrow and winding lane with deep marsh either side. They were soon stopped by a three-gun battery of Confederate artillery with supporting infantry, however. In his official report of the action, Porter recorded:

> We immediately manned the drag ropes and advanced about 2 miles, when I received an order from General Foster to bring the battery forward as fast as possible ... As soon as I saw the enemy's fortification I halted and ... opened fire ... with grape and shell from the rifled guns, and canister, shrapnel, and shell from the smooth bore ... As I had received orders to keep the artillery on a line with the infantry, I advanced the pieces after each fire until they were in the open space directly in front of the rebel battery, where we made a stand under a most destructive fire from the rebel infantry. The men, however, worked the guns with great coolness and determination. (*ORs*, I.6: 579)

Following flanking attacks by Reno's and Parke's brigades, the Confederates were driven back and forced to seek refuge in their coastal forts, following which they surrendered. Afterwards, Foster gave a tribute of commendation, stating: "I would notice here the gallant conduct of Midshipman Benjamin H. Porter ... who commanded the light guns from the ships' launches, and was constantly under fire" (*ORs*, I.9: 88).

The capture of Roanoke Island opened up eastern North Carolina to Union invasion. By the summer of 1862, the port cities of Plymouth, Elizabeth City, New Bern, Washington, Edenton, and Hertford in North Carolina, plus Norfolk, Virginia, were under Union control and largely remained so until the end of the Civil War.

NEW BERN, MARCH 11–14, 1862

Following success at Roanoke Island, the Union Navy entered Albemarle Sound and destroyed much of the Confederate Mosquito Fleet in the Pasquotank River. As a result, Elizabeth City was captured on February 10, 1862. After the capture of Edenton farther down Albemarle Sound, the combined Union force turned its attention on New Bern, which lay on the southwest bank of the Neuse River, about 37 miles above its exit into Pamlico Sound. The Neuse was broad and deep enough to allow vessels to ply up the river. Although replaced in importance by Morehead City and Beaufort by the 1860s, New Bern was still a significant military target as the Atlantic and North Carolina Railroad, opened in 1858, passed through the city and connected the coast with the interior. It also crossed the Wilmington and Weldon Railroad, which was becoming increasingly more important as a lifeline for the Confederacy. Thus, if New Bern fell to the Union Army, an important link in the supply chain of the Confederate forces in Virginia would be threatened.

Brigadier General Burnside's Navy counterpart in operations against New Bern would be Commodore Stephen Rowan, as Flag Officer Goldsborough had been had been called to Hampton Roads to assist in responding to the threat posed by the Confederate Navy's first ironclad CSS *Virginia*.

The soldiers of the Coast Division, consisting of three brigades amounting to approximately 11,000 men, embarked on their Army transports at Roanoke Island on March 11, 1862, and got underway at 0730hrs the next

Produced by Private Herbert E. Valentine, Co. G, 23d Massachusetts Infantry, this painting depicts the advance of the Union Navy gunboats up the Neuse River to New Bern on March 14, 1862. Being bypassed are sunken Confederate hulks meant to form a barrier across the river. (Record Group 165, Herbert Eugene Valentine's sketches of Civil War Scenes, US National Archives)

The advance of the Gunboats up the river to New Berne N.C. Passing the Barricade Mch. 14

Commanding *Pawnee*, Stephen C. Rowan assisted in the capture of the forts at Hatteras Inlet in August 1861. As executive officer of *Delaware*, he participated in the capture of Roanoke Island. He commanded the Navy gunboats at New Bern on March 11–14, 1862. Photographed at the New York City studio of Mathew B. Brady, he wears the sleeve lace of a captain but was appointed to the rank of flag officer with the courtesy title of commodore in 1862. (US National Archives NWDNS-111-B-4517)

morning accompanied by 14 Navy gunboats, and several Army gunboats. By 1300hrs the fleet had passed the mouth of the Pamlico River and reached Brant Island. By 1410hrs the advance division of gunboats had entered the mouth of the Neuse River and was signaled to stop by Rowan in order that the fleet might be kept together. At this point, Burnside came alongside the Navy steamer *Philadelphia*, Rowan's flagship, in the Army transport *Samuel R. Spaulding* and requested that a Navy vessel might be sent to the mouth of the Pamlico to guard against the possibility of the expedition being cut off, as two Confederate steamers had been spotted in that river. As a result, Rowan ordered the Navy steamer *John L. Lockwood* to anchor off the mouth of the Pamlico that night.

Joining the advance division of gunboats by 1540hrs, Rowan issued the signal "form line ahead," and the entire fleet steamed up the Neuse River in two columns (*ORNs*, I.7: 110). By 1700hrs, the gunboats spied the sunken hulks and torpedoes, or floating explosive devices, placed across the river opposite their shore batteries by the Confederates. At 1810hrs the fleet hove to off Slocum's Creek, which was the point chosen for the debarkation of troops, being about 15 miles south of New Bern.

Early in the morning of March 13, Rowan placed the Navy gunboats *Stars and Stripes* and *Louisiana* on the west side of Slocum's Creek, and *Hetzel* and *Valley City* on the east side. At 0630hrs, Burnside hoisted a "preparatory signal" flag and the Army gunboat *Picket* moved in toward the mouth of the creek to shell the woods behind the landing place on the northern bank of the creek, while a skiff from the gunboat *Delaware* was rowed in to ascertain the depth of water (*ORs*, I.9: 208). After receiving a positive report at about 0700hrs, the signal for landing was hoisted and light-draught steamers crammed with troops towing surfboats containing more men headed for the shore. Where possible, the steamers were to approach as close as possible, permitting the men to jump into the waist-deep water and, holding their cartridge boxes above their heads, wade ashore. Carrying up to 70 men each, the surfboats had little trouble in beaching, following which the troops hardly got wet feet.

In his after-action report, Colonel Thomas G. Stevenson, commanding the 24th Massachusetts Infantry, of Foster's 1st Brigade, stated: "I received the signal to prepare to land, and ... filled the boats belonging to my transports with a part of my men and fastened them to the stern of the steamer Pilot Boy, which came alongside the [transport] Guide and took the companies that remained on her" (*ORs*, I.9: 217). Commanding the 27th Massachusetts Infantry, Colonel Horace C. Lee reported: "we commenced landing troops, one company at a time (which was all the

boat would accommodate), from ... the [transports] Recruit and Ranger" (*ORs*, I.9: 219).

Not all went as smoothly for other units, however. Colonel Edward Ferrero reported that the landing of his regiment, the 51st New York Infantry, from the transports *Lancer* and *Pioneer*, was obstructed by "spiles," or wooden spikes, driven into the riverbed (*ORs*, I.9: 229). Similarly, Brigadier General Parke recorded that the 11th Connecticut Infantry, commanded by Lieutenant Colonel Charles Mathewson, found "obstructions in the mouth of the creek," which meant their steamer was "unable to reach the bank, and the men were landed in small boats; an operation consuming much time" (*ORs*, I.9: 233).

Also landed were six Navy boat-howitzers and their crews, commanded by Lieutenant Roderick S. McCook of *Stars and Stripes*. Some of the gunners under McCook's command were from the 99th New York Infantry, or Union Coast Guard, and their steel 12-pounder boat-howitzers were of the Wiard pattern.

Unchallenged by the Confederates, Burnside's troops began marching north along the riverbank at 1130hrs. Meanwhile, Rowan's gunboats proceeded up the Neuse in advance of the Union infantry, throwing shot and shell into the woodland to dissuade any opposition, but the enemy had fallen back to Fort Dixie and its main line of defense beyond. At sundown the firing ceased, and the fleet anchored in position to cover the troops bivouacked ashore.

The fighting resumed at 0630hrs on March 14, and shortly afterward Fort Dixie was found to have been abandoned by the Confederates. Launches from the fleet landed and sailors planted the "Stars and Stripes"

Entitled "The Battle at Newbern – Repulse of the Rebels, March 14, 1863," this engraving was published in *Harper's Weekly* on April 11, 1863. It depicts the action at Fort Anderson on the Neuse River. The Navy gunboats *Hunchback*, *Hetzel*, *Ceres*, and *Shawsheen* are firing from the river at Confederate forces, as Union artillery and infantry move into position on the near shore. (Naval History and Heritage Command NH 95121)

This pen-and-wash illustration by Private Herbert E. Valentine, Co. F, 23d Massachusetts Infantry, shows the gunboat *Ranger*, a converted Hudson River boat. Commanded by Captain John B. Childs, the gunboat had an oak-plank barricade built all around its sides from lower deck to the hurricane roof, with gun-ports and musket loopholes cut through. *Ranger* transported elements of the 27th Massachusetts Infantry during the landings at New Bern on March 13, 1862. (MOLLUS-Massachusetts Civil War Photograph Collection, Volume 131, p 6743)

on the fort's ramparts. Continuing their advance in heavy rain, the troops of Foster's 1st Brigade approached Fort Thompson and its extended lines of breastworks. At this point, McCook's battery was ordered forward in support of the 23d, 24th, 25th, and 27th Massachusetts Infantry. His battery was dragged within 600yd of the enemy line and held their position for 1½ hours before being forced back under heavy fire from muskets and field artillery, having one gun disabled.

Finally seeing the Confederates retreating from their rifle pits, McCook again pressed forward in support of the infantry. Reaching a railroad track, the Union forces captured elements of the 25th North Carolina Infantry, commanded by Colonel Clark M. Avery, which were trying to escape. Ordered to advance north into New Bern along the railroad track, McCook placed his guns on two rail cars and reached New Bern to find the US Navy in possession of the city and the gunboats transporting troops across the Trent River because the railroad bridge had been destroyed. In his after-battle report, McCook praised his men for "dragging their guns through the heavy roads, part of the time exposed to a drenching rain" (*ORN*s, I.7: 113).

Following the Union victory at New Bern, Burnside turned his attention to Beaufort and Fort Macon, the final objectives of his campaign in eastern North Carolina, New Bern became the headquarters of the Union occupying forces and remained so throughout the remainder of the Civil War, despite several Confederate attempts to retake it.

THE 1st NEW YORK MARINE ARTILLERY, 1862–63

In order to support and cooperate with naval operations probing the estuaries and rivers along the North Carolina coastline, and to conduct raids on cities and communities inland, a specialist unit designated the 1st New York Marine Artillery was organized under the command of Colonel William A. Howard during 1861–62.

According to a report in the *New York Times*, this regiment was based on "the principle of the Royal Marine Artillery, one of the crack regiments in the British army," which manned mortars in bomb vessels and light guns during amphibious assaults (*NYT*, September 19, 1862: 2.6). A unit of the volunteer Army rather than the Navy, the 1st New York Marine Artillery was recruited in New York City and Buffalo, New York; Newark, New Jersey; Chicago, Illinois; and Washington, DC. Recruits were mustered-in for three years and advised: "The regiment serves in gunboats and work their artillery on shore or on board, as may be required, throwing the guns overboard and hauling them to land, or the reverse, as wanted" (*NYT*, September 19, 1862: 2.6). Recruiting notices in Chicago stated further that landsmen, meaning those without previous sea service, would have "nothing to do with working the vessel," but would be employed as "riflemen and heavy artillery" (*CDT*, July 18, 1862: 1.7).

On April 18–19, 1862, the 1st New York Marine Artillery formed part of an expedition to destroy a lock at the lower end of the Dismal Swamp Canal, about 8 miles north of Camden Court House, North Carolina, thereby cutting off and capturing Confederate troops stationed south of that point. Commanded by Brigadier General Reno, the Union force included two Wiard 12-pounder boat-howitzers manned by the 1st New York Marine Artillery under the command of Colonel Howard. Pursuing an enemy withdrawal, Reno's infantry encountered a Confederate force in dense woodland at South Mills, a few miles south of the Dismal Swamp Canal and, after being dragged and manhandled through mud and ditches, 1st New York Marine Artillery guns in charge of First Lieutenant William B. Avery, Co. B, and Second Lieutenant George Gerard, Co. D, were brought into action by their exhausted crews.

According to a reporter for the *New York Daily Tribune* who accompanied the expedition, prior to this

> Col. Howard walked up the center of the road, in front of the enemies [*sic*] battery, until he arrived within musket range, when he very coolly took a survey of their position through his glass, which so confounded them that they hardly knew what to make of this strange and daring move. After satisfying himself as to the number of their guns and their location, he turned and retraced his steps, walking down the center of the road as deliberately as a farmer would return from the labors of the day, neither looking to the right or left, at the shells which were flying in great numbers each side of him, one striking the flap of his coat. (*NYDT*, May 5, 1862: 2.3)

Following "a very hot fire" from Howard's guns, and a supporting infantry attack, the Confederates eventually withdrew their battery and commenced

William A. Howard began his naval career as a midshipman in the US Navy in 1825. In 1837 he received a commission as a captain in the US Revenue Cutter Service. Resigning in 1838, he was appointed to command a vessel in the newly created Navy of the Republic of Texas. By 1844 he was again a captain in the US Revenue Cutter Service, commanding the steam-powered schooner *Legare*. Resigning his commission once more, in 1851 he established a shipping line between the Islands of the Hawaiian Kingdom and California. He was called back into the US Revenue Cutter Service on April 20, 1861, to take charge of arming, equipping, and assigning to stations the revenue vessels, but resigned after being accused of overstepping his authority. Appointed colonel of the 1st New York Marine Artillery on September 1, 1861, he was discharged on March 23, 1863. On May 11, 1863, he was given command of the 13th New York Heavy Artillery, the third battalion of which was designated the Naval Brigade. He was honorably mustered-out of military service on July 4, 1865. (US National Archives 111-B-2785)

a retreat. Although within striking distance of the canal entrance, Reno ordered his force to return to their transports. In his after-battle report, Howard commented: "When it is considered that our men marched nearly all night, fought a hard battle of three hour's duration, and marched the same distance the second night without sleep through deep mud cheerfully, without a murmur, too much praise cannot be awarded them" (*ORs*, I.9: 308–09).

During a further land attack on a Confederate force at Tranter's Creek, near Washington, North Carolina, on June 5, 1862, Avery again commanded a section of two Wiard boat-howitzers manned by a detachment of 24 men drawn from Cos C and G, 1st New York Marine Artillery. Unable to force a crossing of the creek with his infantry, the Union commander, Colonel Thomas J.C. Amory, ordered up Avery's guns, which were pulled forward by their crews through a hail of Confederate small-arms fire. One of the guns was brought to bear on the enemy's front while the other was placed to the left of a bridge from where it raked the enemy's right flank. Avery's guns kept up such a persistent bombardment of grape and shell that they eventually drove the enemy out of the mill buildings on the opposite bank of Tranter's Creek and forced them to withdraw. The 1st New York Marine Artillery gun crews sustained one killed and three wounded during this action, with gun captain Sergeant William H. Moore, Co. C, receiving a fatal gunshot wound through the chest. Moore's dying words were reported to be: "My God, my country and my flag. Boys do your duty!" (*NWP*, June 14, 1862: 1.6).

In recognition of his success at Roanoke Island and New Bern, Burnside was promoted to major general and transferred to Virginia during July 1862, with many of his troops being transported north to Newport News, following which they joined the ranks of his IX Corps, Army of the Potomac. Meanwhile, the 1st New York Marine Artillery continued to serve on the

FAR LEFT
One of 282 men from Chicago, Illinois, to enlist in the 1st New York Marine Artillery, Andrew Wenz, alias Wenc, was mustered-in as a private in Co. G of the regiment on July 30, 1862. His uniform consists of a plain dark-blue Navy cap, plain dark-blue jacket with two rows of five buttons and three buttons on each cuff, and plain matching trousers. His tall boots suggest he may have been involved in landing operations involving mounted action. Wenz was honorably discharged on January 25, 1863, at New Bern, or Hilton Head, North Carolina. (Author's collection)

LEFT
A house or sign painter by occupation residing in Ossining, Westchester County, New York, William Knight enlisted in New York City in Co. E, 1st New York Marine Artillery, on January 23, 1862. He died of disease at the regimental hospital at New Bern on October 19, 1862. (Author's collection)

North Carolina coast with approximately half the regiment garrisoning Roanoke Island, and the remainder based at New Bern. Operating from Roanoke Island, the unit also mounted amphibious expeditions to destroy Confederate salt works along the coast near Carrituck Court House and Swansboro. Elsewhere, launches and armed steamers under Howard's command plied up and down the estuaries of the Perquimans and Chowan

The 1st New York Marine Artillery in action at Tranter's Creek, North Carolina, on June 5, 1862. The two Wiard boat-howitzers commanded by First Lieutenant William B. Avery are shown discharging shell and canister at the Confederates, while infantry of the 24th Massachusetts Infantry's advance under cover of their fire. Elements of the 1st New York Marine Artillery were most successful in land engagements such as this. This engraving was published in *Harper's Weekly* on June 28, 1862. (Author's collection)

Based on a sketch by Angelo Wiser, this line engraving published in *Harper's Weekly* on July 19, 1862, shows 1st New York Marine Artillery gun teams pulling their 12-pounder boat-howitzers during a parade in Washington, North Carolina, in honor of the arrival of Brigadier General Edward W. Stanly as the military governor of Union-occupied North Carolina on May 26, 1862. (Author's collection)

rivers in order to break up trade with Richmond, Virginia. In his memoir, Avery recalled:

> In operating with the army, our most effective weapon was the howitzer, we acting as a field battery; but when making strikes by ourselves, often at some of the guerrillas, we generally went light, with only rifles or pistols. Sometimes making forced loans of horses we rode, or if at night, and the distance to be covered was short, we went on foot, and generally returned to our boat without making any halt at all. (Avery 1880: 9)

An incident during an attack on a Confederate battery near Swift Creek Village, about 12 miles north of New Bern on June 26, 1862, reveals that the 1st New York Marine Artillery was not altogether comfortable commandeering horses or mules to pull their guns. Tasked with clearing the way for further probes along the Neuse toward Kinston and Goldsboro, the Union force consisted of the 17th Massachusetts Infantry, 3d New York Cavalry, and 300 men of the 1st New York Marine Artillery with ten field pieces. After all five of the vessels involved in the expedition became stuck on the riverbed about 3 miles upstream from New Bern, three guns and their crews of the 1st New York Marine Artillery, commanded by Captain Caleb C. Eyre, Co. B, were landed at the mouth of the narrow Swift Creek, and advanced rapidly overland toward their objective. After an exchange of musketry fire, the Confederate garrison withdrew after shots from one of the guns smashed through the shingle breastworks of their unfinished battery,

C **THE 1ST NEW YORK MARINE ARTILLERY AT SWIFT CREEK VILLAGE, JUNE 26, 1862**

In action with a landing party, the Wiard boat-howitzer was pulled and pushed along by a 12-man team using a drag rope attached to the small wheel on the gun trail. Magazine boxes carrying shells and fuses were strapped above the axle either side of the gun tube. Each man, except the gun captain and second gun captain, carried a leather pouch or pass box over his right shoulder containing one round for the gun. The strap of the pouch was as short as possible so as to keep the ammunition clear of the water when leaving the boat.

allowing the 1st New York Marine Artillery with supporting infantry and cavalry to sweep into Swift Creek Village beyond.

During the following hours, Union foragers brought in horses and mules to pull the three guns, and a *New York Daily Tribune* reporter with the expedition described the "grand business of harnessing," which was basically incompatible with the trail wheel system on the Wiard boat-howitzers, as follows:

> Every strap and buckle seemed to have got in its wrong place, and "all fingers were thumbs." By some the breechings would be viewed as Dutch collars, and put over the horse's neck; while others would vainly attempt to buckle the harness on upside down, and make the girths fit the place where the saddle should have been. Some, in despair, would give up the job as a bad one, and damn the horses and "horse tackle" in the roughest of expletives. (*NYDT*, July 8, 1862: 1.4)

Alarmed at the strength of a struggling mule, one man exclaimed, "Avast there! Make him fast, men; he's adrift." Impressed by the braying of the animal, they named it "The Bugler" and appointed it the "Child of the Regiment" (*NYDT*, July 8, 1862: 1.4).

The action near Shiloh, North Carolina, on September 19–20, 1862, offers a further example of the 1st New York Marine Artillery's use of horses and mules. As the result of a successful Confederate guerrilla raid on the encampment of the 1st North Carolina (Union) Infantry at a hamlet called Old Trap, during which seven prisoners were taken and a howitzer captured, the Army gunboat *Lancer*, commanded by Avery, was ordered up the Tar River to the vicinity. Landing a force of 60 men from Cos E and G, 1st New York Marine Artillery, Avery requisitioned several mule carts and chased after the guerrillas. Eventually catching up with them near Hinton's Corner, Pasquotank County, his command dashed after their prey in what became known as the Cart Charge. The guerrillas escaped into the swampland without firing a shot, however, and the prisoners and small arms were recovered, but the howitzer was never retrieved (*ORs*, I.18: 14–15).

The 1st New York Marine Artillery's last main action occurred on December 10–14, 1862, during an unsuccessful expedition toward Kinston on the Neuse River that involved three Navy gunboats and five steamers manned by the 1st New York Marine Artillery under Lieutenant Colonel Horace A. Manchester. Owing to low water, the Navy vessels were unable to steam more than 18 miles inland and, as a result, the 1st New York Marine Artillery flotilla with shallower draft proceeded alone. Surprised by an 11-gun Confederate battery as it rounded a point of land within 2 miles of Kinston, the lead vessel, the tug gunboat *Allison*, was repeatedly struck by shot and shell. Unable to turn due to the narrowness of the Neuse, *Allison* took about 20 minutes to reverse to safety, being seriously damaged during that time. As the expedition steamed back downstream, Private Edward J. Perkins, Co. E, 1st New York Marine Artillery, was killed aboard the chartered side-wheel steamer *Ocean Wave* by sniper fire from Confederate guerrillas positioned along the riverbank (*PI*, December 22, 1862: 3.4–5).

On March 31, 1863, the 1st New York Marine Artillery was disbanded as a direct result of a mutiny of 150 of its enlisted men during December 1862 over lack of pay and failure to provide promised enlistment bounties and prize money. While at Roanoke Island, these men attempted to seize

This pen-and-wash illustration by Private Herbert E. Valentine, Co. F, 23d Massachusetts Infantry, shows the Army gunboat *Pioneer*. Another converted Hudson River tugboat, *Pioneer* was at the center of a mutiny during December 1862 when disgruntled enlisted men of the 1st New York Marine Artillery unsuccessfully attempted to seize control of the vessel. As a result, the regiment was disbanded several months later and the imprisoned mutineers were forced to transfer to other units. (MOLLUS-Massachusetts Civil War Photograph Collection, Vol. 131, p 6743)

control of the Army gunboat *Pioneer*. Although the mutiny was solely the action of enlisted personnel, a number of the regiment's officers were held responsible. One company-grade officer, Captain Edward C. Bowers, was subsequently convicted by court-martial for neglect of duty, while Lieutenant Colonel Manchester was dismissed from the service.

Despite the scandal, Colonel Howard was not considered at fault and, according to Brigadier General Foster, the 1st New York Marine Artillery had been "an essential part of all coastwise expeditions" (*Documents* 1863: 461).

THE NAVAL BATTALION, 13th NEW YORK HEAVY ARTILLERY, 1863–64

Following the disbandment of the 1st New York Marine Artillery, Colonel Howard – its former commander – was authorized on May 11, 1863, to recruit the 13th New York Heavy Artillery, which included a "Battalion of Sailors" composed of 600 seaman, ordinary seamen, boatmen, and landsmen officially designated as Cos I, K, L, and M (*TW*, August 21, 1863: 8.4). Recruiting for this amphibious unit began in New York City during August 1863, and continued in Buffalo, New York, in February 1864, under Captain J. Travis Sweet, ex-captain of Co. K, 1st New York Marine Artillery, and Captain John A. Bloomer, ex-first lieutenant, Co. F, 1st New York Marine Artillery, respectively. Recruits were advised that "Sailor clothing" would be issued (*TW*, August 21, 1863: 8.6).

Although the first two battalions of the 13th New York Heavy Artillery served as garrison troops and siege artillery in the Third Division, XVIII Corps, Army of the James, the four companies of the third battalion, also known as the Naval Battalion, or Naval Brigade, were placed under

All Hands on Deck!

Wanted Immediately for the
13th N. Y. S. ARTILLERY !

Seamen, Ordinary Seamen, Boatmen, Landsmen, for the expedition under command of

COL. WM. A. HOWARD.

Now being rapidly fitted out in New York, FOR SERVICE IN THE SOUNDS AND INLAND WATERS OF THE SOUTH.

These splendid new Gun Boats will carry six Rifled Wiard Guns each, and all other Arms the same as the Navy.

All Bounties Paid by the U. S. States and County.

Added to the advantages of being on Shipboard, make this the most desirable arm of the Service. The uniforms of the Corps will be the same as the Navy. Apply to

Capt. J. A. BLOOMER,
Recruiting Officer.

Office United States Hotel, west side of the Terrace.　　　　　　　　　　　　fe1-1m.

Brigadier General Charles K. Graham. This unit served aboard Army steamboats with company-grade officers commanding, and crews made up of Naval Battalion personnel plus some civilians.

The light-draught transport vessels aboard which the Naval Battalion served were of "an entire new pattern" built under the supervision of Norman Wiard (*TW*, August 21, 1863: 8.4). Built by the Continental Iron Works, at Greenpoint, Brooklyn, New York City, each of these six vessels was 150ft in length, with a 21ft beam, 7ft depth, and 200 tons burthen. Powered by inclined engines developed by Wiard, their light draught enabled them to operate in only 3ft 6in of water while carrying 800 troops plus coal and stores. Carrying Wiard boat-howitzers, their gunwales were protected by bulletproof iron plating and had a bulletproof pilothouse. A news report claimed, "They can be turned completely around in the space of their own length, and will run either end foremost with equal facility" (*BSWA*, December 14, 1864: 1.8).

Although serving the same purpose as those used by the Mississippi Marine Brigade on the Western Rivers since March 1863, the six vessels were side-wheelers and double-enders capable of steaming in either direction along narrow rivers without the need to turn. Received by the beginning of 1864, they consisted of *General Burnside*, *General Reno*, *General Parke*, and *General Foster* (*ORs*, I.35.2: 167). The double-ender *Augusta* and *Savannah* were completed toward the end of 1864 and saw limited service during the final months of the war transporting troops between New York and Virginia (*SORs*, II.39: 305). Other vessels used by Graham's Naval Battalion were the Army side-wheel steamer *Charles Chamberlain*, which was stationed in the James River, Virginia, and used by Graham as his flagship, plus *Samuel L. Brewster*, *Flora Temple*, and *General Jessup* (*DOS*, May 11, 1864: 2.3).

From 1863 through 1865, Graham coordinated a series of amphibious operations that penetrated the estuaries and coastal rivers of Virginia and North Carolina, and did much to disrupt the Confederate cause. The tactics used included daring raids using rowed or sail-rigged launches, each about

42ft in length and accommodating about 25–30 men, and carrying Wiard boat-howitzers. In a letter written aboard *Charles Chamberlain* in the Appomattox River, Virginia, and dated October 21, 1864, a sailor who signed himself only as "Will" stated: "There are no less than fifty launches laying here for this Brigade ... we are drilled in rowing them twice a day" (*DEE*, October 29, 1864: 2.5).

Stationed off Norfolk, Virginia, and commanded by Captain Robert W. McLaughlin and crewed by Co. I, Naval Battalion, *General Foster* mounted several raids along the Alligator River toward Fairfield, North Carolina, which was occupied by a small Confederate force. During a snowstorm on February 16, 1864, elements of the Naval Battalion, plus a detachment of the 101st Pennsylvania Infantry, attacked Fairfield in launches towed partway by *General Foster*. An after-battle report stated: "The camp was surprised, the arms and stores secured and the whole company taken prisoners, without loss on our side" (*NYDH*, March 31, 1864: 2.6).

On April 14, 1864, Co. K, Naval Battalion, Captain John S. Gordon commanding, took part in a raid along the Pagan River toward Smithfield, Virginia, in response to a torpedo-boat attack on the screw frigate *Minnesota* four days earlier. According to local informants, the torpedo, or floating contact mine, had been at Smithfield for several days before it was towed down to the James River. The Naval Battalion expedition made landings at three locations and engaged in several fierce firefights with Confederate troops. As a result, two men were killed and eight were wounded. Included in the former was Navy Lieutenant Charles B. Wilder, executive officer of *Minnesota*, who had command of the launches despite having one arm in a sling, having been wounded in action 16 days before. According to a news report, he was shot through the head while attempting to land his launch and was in "the act of sighting the gun" (*TDA*, April 20, 1864: 2.4).

Anchored in the James River off Herring Creek, the crew of the gunboat *Parke* observed enemy activity along the riverbank to the north on July 16, 1864. Captain Amasa L. Fitch led ashore a detachment of 25 men of Co. L, Naval Battalion, and drove about 50 Confederate troops off. Bivouacking for the night, Fitch sent out scouts the next morning and discovered in the bushes overhanging the riverbank two light boats, which had been carted from Richmond and launched in Herring Creek. These contained 12 torpedoes, each containing about 150lb of explosives complete with

Possibly an enlisted man of the Naval Battalion, 13th New York Heavy Artillery, this volunteer wears a sailor's cap with waterproof cover and blue shirt or Army sack coat tucked into fly-front trousers. His belt has an oval "SNY" plate and revolver attached via a leather frog. (Author's collection)

Photographed near Point of Rocks on the Appomattox River, Virginia, the crew of US Army gunboat *General Foster*, composed of Co. I, Naval Battalion, man a battery of four Wiard boat-howitzers in 1864. (Library of Congress LC-DIG-cwpb-02029 DLC)

anchors, grapples, and percussion apparatus. A newspaper report of this action concluded that further attempts to attack Union gunboats had been "frustrated by the vigilance and promptness of the army gunboat Parke" (*CDT*, July 23, 1864: 3.5).

Off New Bern, aboard *General Reno*, a detachment of 60 men of Co. K, Naval Battalion, under Captain Gordon, set off in three launches up the Neuse at 0200hrs on October 7, 1864. Reaching the mouth of Swift Creek, a section of men landed, engaged in a firefight with Confederate pickets, and drove them off. Having received reinforcements, the Confederates renewed contact and during the action Gordon, the company commander and executive officer of *General Reno*, was "shot in the right breast and expired immediately" (*BDWC*, November 5, 1864: 2.2–3). In his after-action report, Second Lieutenant Stewart J. Donnelly, who assumed command of *General Reno*, stated: "The enemy being superior to our detachment in number, we retired to our boats, destroying on the way one picket station and several boats" (*SORs*, II.42: 88).

D **LAUNCHES AND HOWITZERS**

(1) Ground plan of an armed ship's launch
The armed launch used by the US Navy and amphibious units developed by the US Army was 8ft wide, 30ft long, and 3ft in depth. It had three pivot sockets (**1a**) at the bow and three more at the stern to which the boat-howitzer (**1b**) mounted on a sliding carriage (**1c**) could be pivoted from port to starboard bow. Two tracks (**1d**) the width of the field carriage (**1e**) ran fore and aft. Two skids, with hooks at the ends to fix in eyes at the bow and stern, enabled the tracks to be slid down on to the beach or riverbank to support the field carriage when landing.

A total of 16 oars were available for use by the oarsmen. The oars had India rubber tubing slipped over them, and each oar rested on a piece of rubber let into the gunwale to muffle their sound. The gun captain (**1f**) pointed and fired the gun, superintended orders, and gave orders in the absence of an officer, while the second gun captain (**1g**) tended the vent and primed the gun. The second oar starboard side (**1h**) sponged the boat-howitzer and pushed home the charge, and the second oar port side (**1i**) received and loaded the ammunition. The third oar starboard side (**1j**) tended the forward compressor, while the third oar port side (**1k**) tended the after

compressor; the fourth oar starboard side (**1l**) tended the train rope. The ninth oar starboard side (**1m**) and ninth oar port side (**1n**) ran the field carriage forward when landing. Finally, the coxswain (**1o**) tended the helm and the quartermaster (**1p**) was responsible for signals and assisted with ammunition.

Stowed away were 12 pass boxes, and each member of the gun crew carried one round of ammunition on landing. Also carried were two watertight copper magazine tanks, to which a line could be attached. When a launch was under fire the magazines were dropped overboard, and towed 5 or 10 fathoms (30 or 60ft) behind. When performing a beach or riverbank landing, two grapnels with 30 fathoms (180ft) of line were thrown overboard before the boat met the surf, breaking waves, or marsh so that the launch could be hauled off as soon as the boat-howitzer and its crew were landed.

(2) Boat-howitzer on sliding carriage
The boat-howitzer consisted of a bed (**2a**) and a slide (**2b**), clamped together with compressor handles (**2c**). The boat-howitzer's barrel fitted into a pair of lugs (**2d**). Not shown in this drawing are the compressor plate and bolts.

(3) Armed ship's launch in action
This launch is crewed by elements of the Naval Battalion, 13th New York Heavy Artillery, in 1864.

1a   1a   1n   1d   1k   1i   1g   1b   1a   1p   1e   1c   1f   1o   1a   1d   1m   1l   1j   1h   1a

1

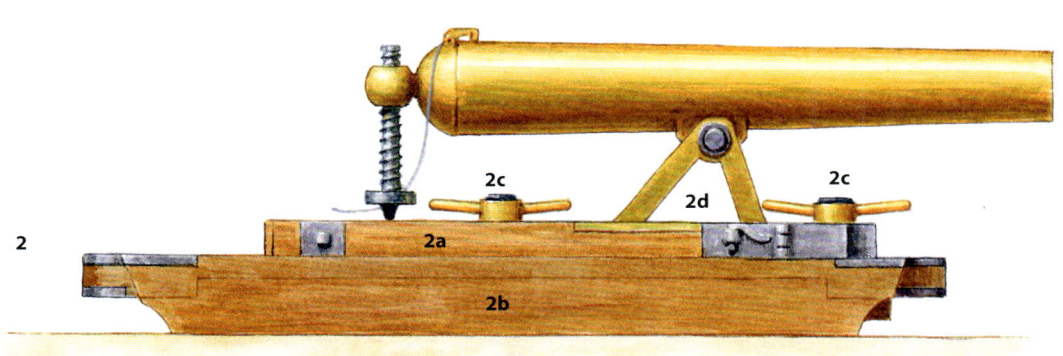

2   2c   2c   2d   2a   2b

3

THE MISSISSIPPI MARINE BRIGADE, 1862–64

Beginning the war as captain of Co. I, 9th Missouri Infantry, Alfred W. Ellet fought at the battle of Pea Ridge on March 7–8, 1862, following which his brother Colonel Charles Ellet, Jr., created and took command of the United States Ram Fleet. Given command of the ram *Monarch*, Alfred Ellet became second-in-command of the Ram Fleet with the rank of lieutenant colonel. On November 1, 1862, he was promoted to brigadier general and charged with creation of the Mississippi Marine Brigade. (Dennis Hood Collection)

Hiram G. Parker originally enlisted in the 10th Illinois Infantry, and transferred to the Mississippi Marine Brigade in January 1863 serving as a private in Co. B, Marine Infantry Regiment, aboard the flagship *Autocrat*. (Paul Russinoff collection)

With increased guerrilla warfare and attacks on gunboats and military transports on the Western Rivers, a need for a specialist amphibious fighting force became apparent to the War Department by the fall of 1862. When Rear Admiral David D. Porter took command of the Upper Mississippi Squadron on October 9, he applied for a force of Marines to be carried in suitable vessels accompanying his gunboats, but the Navy Department refused his request. As a result, on November 1, 1862, a directive was issued to Brigadier General Alfred W. Ellet by Secretary of War Edwin M. Stanton to form the Mississippi Marine Brigade for service aboard vessels alongside the Mississippi Ram Fleet, which had been organized in March 1862 by Colonel Charles Ellet, Jr., elder brother of Alfred Ellet. Since the death of Charles, who was mortally wounded at the first battle of Memphis on June 6, 1862, Alfred Ellet had served as Flag Officer of the Ram Fleet.

To be composed of infantry, cavalry, and light artillery, the Mississippi Marine Brigade, also originally known as Ellet's Scouts, began to organize at St. Louis, Missouri, and other western cities during December 1862. A recruiting agent in New Albany, Indiana, declared: "It is certainly the most desirous arm of the service, as the soldier never has any marching to do; no knapsack to carry, is never without a comfortable place to sleep and always plenty to eat" (*WD*, December 10, 1862: 3.1).

Recruiting handbills were initially distributed in Army hospitals in St. Louis in the hopes that volunteers would be gained among convalescing soldiers, who were offered a $100 bounty upon enlistment. With insufficient numbers enlisted via this means or any other by February 11, 1863, however, Secretary of War Stanton authorized via Special Order No. 69 the permanent transfer into the Mississippi Marine Brigade of detachments from the 59th and 63d Illinois Infantry, plus Co. K, 18th Illinois Infantry, which already served aboard the Ram Fleet (Crandall & Newell 1907: 166).

To accommodate the men of the Mississippi Marine Brigade, and their horses, the War Department purchased the steamers *Autocrat*, *Ben J. Adams*, *Baltic*, *Diana*, and *John Raine*, which were converted into armed transports. *Autocrat* served as the flagship, *E.H. Fairchild* was fitted out as a quartermaster and commissary boat, and *Woodford* as a hospital boat. Smaller vessels serving with the Mississippi Marine Brigade as tugboats and towboats included *Lioness*, *T.D. Horner*, *Belle Darlington*, *Alf Cutting*, and *Dick Fulton*. The rams *Switzerland*, *Lancaster*, and *Queen of the West* would also later carry Mississippi Marine Brigade units. While the actual working of each steamer was handled by a civilian crew, many of whom were African-Americans who had escaped slavery, it was commanded by a Mississippi Marine Brigade officer who had authority over both the crew of the steamer and the assault troops assigned to it.

All the larger vessels required extensive refitting. Boilers were protected by heavy timbers. A barricade of solid, 2in-thick oak plank was built all around each vessel from lower deck to the hurricane roof. Through this was cut loopholes for muskets, while large portholes with swinging doors were included for the great guns and ventilation. To protect pilots from enemy gunfire, the pilothouses had semicircular sheets of boilerplate iron installed along the walls. The after-part of the cabin decks on the troop-carrying vessels were converted to officers' quarters, while the forward part served for the men's messroom. Sleeping quarters for the men were on the next deck down, aft of the boilers. All ranks were provided with suitable washrooms, bathrooms, and facilities for washing clothes. Serving as protection against any attempt at boarding, each vessel was provided with a hot-water hose connected to the boiler, and hung where it was available for instant use. Most importantly, on both sides of the prow were winches for hoisting and lowering wide gangways on to the riverbank, which enabled light artillery, cavalry, and infantry to debark rapidly in order to engage speedily with Confederate guerrillas.

Throughout the winter of 1862/63, the Mississippi Marine Brigade was quartered at Benton Barracks in the northwestern outskirts of St. Louis, and trained under First Lieutenant George E. Currie, 59th Illinois Infantry. The six infantry companies were organized as a regiment under 19-year-old Colonel Charles R. Ellet, Alfred Ellet's nephew. Most of these men were mounted on horses or mules, which gave them a high degree of mobility when they landed ashore. Four separate cavalry companies were made part of that original regimental organization but would later become a separate battalion under Major James M. Hubbard. Captain Daniel P. Walling led the Artillery Battery.

During March 1863, a New York City newspaper reported that the uniform of the brigade was to be "like that of the regular service, except the cap is in the shape something nearer the naval model, and a green band with white facings surrounds it" (*TW*, March 13, 1863: 2.1). While the description of the headgear was correct, all enlisted men of the Mississippi Marine Brigade received untrimmed dark-blue eight-button mounted service jackets with cloth shoulder straps, rather than regulation frock coats. The Infantry Regiment was issued with a mixture of Springfield Model 1855, Model 1861, and Model 1863 rifled muskets, while the Cavalry Battalion was armed with Sharps carbines, Colt Army revolvers, and Model 1840 sabers. The Artillery Battery was equipped with six 3in Model 1861 wrought-iron guns with limbers, plus a traveling forge (NARA M-1281, Roll 4: 356; Roll 2: 217–19; Roll 1: 338–47).

Sufficiently organized and trained, the Mississippi Marine Brigade was ordered to parade with other troops in St. Louis on February 21, 1863 (*DMR*, February 20, 1863: 2.2). Totaling 1,035 men, it boarded the steamers and descended the Mississippi arriving at Cairo, Illinois, "with drums beating and colors flying" on March 14, 1863 (*DMR*, March 16, 1863: 1.1).

Entering the Tennessee River on March 24, 1863, the Mississippi Marine Brigade's first major action was on the Duck River, a tributary of the Tennessee, the banks of which were occupied by numerous Confederate guerrillas by 1863 (*ORN*s, I.23: 396). At about 0800hrs on April 26, while the Army gunboats were negotiating the Duck River Shoals at the mouth of the river, they were fired on by the 6th Texas Cavalry, plus artillery, commanded by Major Robert M. White. The Confederates likely believed they were attacking unarmed transport vessels. During an action that lasted only a few moments, *Autocrat* was struck nine times with solid shot, while the vessel's pilothouse, Texas deck, and hull were peppered with musket balls. *Diana* received six shots while *B.J. Adams* was struck twice. The Confederates quickly realized their mistake when the Mississippi Marine Brigade artillery and sharpshooters threw open the gun-ports and musket loopholes and returned fire.

About 2 miles south of the Duck River Shoals, Mississippi Marine Brigade amphibious tactics were successfully employed for the first time when Colonel

William R. Houts enlisted as a private in Co. A, Marine Infantry Regiment, Mississippi Marine Brigade, on January 14, 1863. He wears the mounted service-pattern jacket issued to the Mississippi Marine Brigade, and his broad-topped cap with green band rests on the photographer's table. (Paul Russinoff collection)

Joseph W. Imhoff was from DeSoto, Illinois, and originally enlisted in Co. K, 18th Illinois Infantry and served as a 4th Engineer with the Ram Fleet aboard *Queen of the West*, *Switzerland*, and *Monarch* before being transferred with his company to the Mississippi Marine Brigade on February 11, 1863. He died of yellow fever in October 1864. (Paul Russinoff collection)

Purchased by the US Army Quartermaster Department in December 1862, the 862-ton armed side-wheel steamer *Autocrat* became the flagship of the Mississippi Marine Brigade in 1863. This engraving based on a sketch by Frank B. Schell was published in *Frank Leslie's Illustrated Newspaper* on August 1, 1863. (Author's collection)

Ellet sounded the whistle signal to land, and the cranes fore and aft on *Autocrat* were lowered to swing the wide gangways ashore, following which elements of the Cavalry Battalion crossed to the riverbank and pursued the attackers, who were already mounted and making a hasty retreat through the thick woods and miry, overgrown swamps. Several infantry companies from *Diana* and *B.J. Adams* were likewise landed but took no part in the pursuit.

Several times the Mississippi Marine Brigade cavalry overtook and fought with the rearguard of the escaping Confederates, but could not force them to make a stand. As they were outnumbered by the retreating enemy, and the Mississippi Marine Brigade infantry although also mounted was left far behind, the chase was abandoned when about 12 miles from the point of the original river attack, and Ellet ordered his troops to return to their gunboats.

In concluding his after-action report, Ellet wrote: "The enemy abandoned their dead, 8 in number, and we buried them. Their wounded they succeeded in carrying off with them, owing to the necessary delay occasioned in landing my troops, from the unfavorable condition of the river banks, and the narrowness of the river at the spot. Our loss was 2 killed and several wounded, only one seriously" (*ORNs*, I.24: 530).

During a similar action on May 23, while the flotilla was steaming down the Mississippi River to Vicksburg, Mississippi, about 200 men of Ellet's Cavalry Battalion were landed near Austin, Mississippi, to pursue Arkansas and Mississippi partisan troops who had fired on the commissary boat *E.H. Fairchild*, which had fallen behind. During the ensuing two-hour action the horsemen were cut off but managed to fight their way out having sustained two killed and 19 wounded. The town of Austin was burned in retaliation for pro-Confederate support, which helped engender considerable hatred for the Mississippi Marine Brigade in the South (*ORs*, I.24: 431).

E "HORSE MARINES" AT THE DUCK RIVER SHOALS, APRIL 26, 1863

Mississippi Marine Brigade amphibious tactics were successfully employed for the first time at the Duck River Shoals, Tennessee, on April 26, 1863, when Brigadier General Alfred W. Ellet ordered the steamboat whistle signal sounded aboard the armed side-wheel steamer and flagship *Autocrat* to land troops of his Cavalry Battalion to pursue elements of the 6th Texas Cavalry, plus artillery, commanded by Major Robert M. White. The winches on the forecastle of *Autocrat* were rapidly lowered to swing gangways ashore, following which elements of the "Horse Marines" crossed to the riverbank and pursued the Confederates, who made a hasty retreat through the thick woods and miry, overgrown swamps of Tennessee.

The Mississippi Marine Brigade saw extensive service in Major General Ulysses S. Grant's Vicksburg Campaign, and during the course of the siege, some of the unit served as sharpshooters. On June 14, 1863, Ellet had a large square pit dug behind and partly into the levee opposite Vicksburg, and ordered Captain Isaac D. Newell, commanding Co. A, Marine Infantry Regiment, to place several men there armed with Spencer long-range rifles, loaned by the Navy, to pick off Confederate details collecting water from the Mississippi River early each morning. During the same month, Lieutenant Colonel Currie supervised the construction of a heavy-artillery battery opposite Vicksburg, called Fort Adams. Under the command of Captain Thomas C. Goshen, Co. F, Marine Infantry Regiment, the battery's guns destroyed an iron foundry on June 25, 1863, which was converting spent Union munitions into useable shot for Confederate guns.

On August 27, 1863, the role of the Mississippi Marine Brigade and its vessels began to be transferred from Navy to Army jurisdiction and duties under Major General Grant. Although Secretary of War Stanton did not approve of Ellet's Marines being converted into "a land brigade," he authorized Grant to use any of them "for temporary shore duty, and any of [Ellet's] boats for temporary transports" whenever required (ORs, I.30.3: 144). As a result, the tactics of the Mississippi Marine Brigade changed to those of landing expeditionary forces to hunt down guerrillas and conduct raids, with less of an emphasis upon amphibious combat operations. This change of tactics was summed up in a Union-supporting Memphis newspaper during the following October as follows:

> Starting from Vicksburg on the 27th of August, they sailed up the river, stopping at various places, dismounting their cavalry force, and scouting the country for a distance of thirty miles. The system of policing the river banks has been as effectual as noble, and the benefits we have realized therefrom are invaluable, furnishing their own fuel in abundance at no cost to the Government, arresting spies, messengers, etc. (MB, October 8, 1863: 4.1)

On September 12, 1863, elements of Cos G and K, Mississippi Marine Brigade, landed from the gunboat *John Raine* at Bolivar Landing, Mississippi, and captured a party of Confederates led by Colonel Trusten W. Polk, Missouri State Guard, who were preparing a sailing yawl to cross the Mississippi River to Arkansas. With Polk was Army paymaster Second Lieutenant John C. Clemson, in charge of $2,500,000 of Confederate scrip, plus 30 other officers and men. Also seized was mail and dispatches from Richmond for Lieutenant General Edmund K. Smith, commanding the Trans-Mississippi Department, which disclosed much about the size and location of the Confederate army in the Midwest. Reporting this action, a New Jersey newspaper commented: "It may be set down as the best and largest haul since Vicksburg" (WJP, October 10, 1863: 1.5).

During November and December 1863, while the Mississippi Marine Brigade was stationed in the Mississippi River opposite Rodney, Mississippi, landing parties captured various other Confederate Army personnel including Captain George E. Price, a commissary agent who had in his possession $12,000 for purchasing livestock for the Confederate Army. They also surprised a Confederate signal station and captured "the entire corps ... together with all their flags and code of signals" (PI, January 8, 1864: 2.1–2).

The Mississippi Marine Brigade continued during the first half of 1864 and conducted a pattern of small-scale operations in Mississippi and Louisiana, confiscating horses, mules, foodstuffs, and valuables. Inevitably, it was responsible for the burning of further Southern property and pillaging goods. For example, at the beginning of June 1864 its troops were among those who torched the town of Columbia, Arkansas, and nearby plantation buildings, in retaliation for Confederate artillery firing on the stern-wheel gunboat *Exchange* (*DES*, June 13, 1864: 2.1).

The last engagement of the Mississippi Marine Brigade took place on June 5, 1864, when it joined elements of the XVII and XXVI Army Corps under Major General Andrew J. Smith and fought an inconclusive battle with a Confederate force under Brigadier General Colton Greene at Ditch Bayou near Lake Village, Arkansas.

The Mississippi Marine Brigade was finally stood down on August 7, 1864, following an inspection by Major General Napoleon J.T. Dana, commander of the District of Vicksburg, which revealed it had become under strength, was without guns or equipment for its artillery, and was using too many vessels during its operations.

THE FLEET BRIGADE, 1863–64

The concept of an amphibious landing force specifically using Union Navy sailors and Marines was put into action by Rear Admiral John Dahlgren, commanding the South Atlantic Blockading Squadron, in July 1863 during the Morris Island siege operations near Charleston, South Carolina. Increasing Union losses combined with the Army's growing fears of Confederate counterattacks spurred Dahlgren into action to help end the siege. He decided to organize a Fleet Brigade of three battalions, one composed of Marines and the other two of sailors, to serve ashore assisting with operations. Commander Foxhall A. Parker commanded the whole force, while Marine Major Jacob Zeilin had charge of the Marine battalion. The Navy Department sent Dahlgren about 260 sailors, while he stripped as many men as possible from his squadron to form the other two battalions (Dahlgren 1892: 400 & 406).

It was the intention to use the whole Fleet Brigade in conjunction with the Army during the attack on Battery Wagner on July 18, 1863, but the sailors were insufficiently trained for light-infantry service ashore and, although the Marines were on station and prepared to participate, the Marine battalion was withdrawn the day before as the three officers available to command them lacked sufficient combat experience.

Men from the Marine battalion, under Captain Charles G. McCawley, plus "a force of sailors for special service," conducted a disastrous boat assault on Fort Sumter, in Charleston Harbor, on September 8, 1863 (*ORN*s, I.14: 606). This action was prompted by the Confederate refusal to

August 23, 1863. Despite persistent bombardment since the beginning of the siege of Charleston that had reduced most of the brick-built Fort Sumter to a pile of rubble, the combined force of Marines and sailors of the Fleet Brigade failed in their assault on September 8, 1863, due to a lack of cooperation between the Navy and Army, and the dogged defense of the Confederate garrison. (Library of Congress LC-DIG-cwpb-04743)

In this engraving, published in *Battles and Leaders of the Civil War* in 1888 and based on a painting by American maritime artist Julian O. Davidson (1853–94), elements of the Fleet Brigade are depicted conducting the unsuccessful boat attack on Fort Sumter in Charleston Harbor on September 8, 1863. (Author's collection)

surrender Charleston following the Union capture of Morris Island the day before. Owing to a lack of communication between the Army and the Navy, Brigadier General Quincy A. Gilmore, commander of the Department of the South, had also planned an Army boat attack on Fort Sumter the same day. On discovering the Navy plan, Gilmore suggested an Army officer should assume overall command of a combined operation, but Dahlgren refused, stating that his Fleet Brigade would not be placed under Army control. Although the two boat attacks proceeded independently, that of the Army was canceled once the alarm had been raised and the Navy attack had failed.

Of 25 Union Navy boats that set out, only 11 managed to land at Fort Sumter. The rest were driven off and returned to the ships of the squadron. Of approximately 400 Marines and sailors who volunteered for the action, eight were killed, 19 wounded, and 105 captured. Following this fiasco, McCawley's Marine battalion went into camp on Folly Island, in Charleston Harbor, where it was stood down in late November 1863. The sailors returned to their respective vessels.

On November 24, 1864, Dahlgren had another opportunity to use a Fleet Brigade when he received a note from Major General Foster requesting naval cooperation to assist with Major General William T. Sherman's "March to the Sea." Two days earlier, Sherman's forces had captured Milledgeville, Georgia, but were still about 150 miles from Savannah, Georgia. Envisioned was a diversionary expedition against the Charleston and Savannah Railroad. If Union forces could destroy this rail line near Grahamville, South Carolina, they might prevent Confederate reinforcements from reaching Savannah and

F | **THE FLEET BRIGADE AT FORT SUMTER, SEPTEMBER 8, 1863**

Sailors and Marines of the Fleet Brigade scramble ashore among the rubble surrounding Fort Sumter on September 8, 1863. An officer turns to urge the men on, while Confederate musketry fire, bricks, hand grenades and fiery turpentine balls, designed to illuminate the target, rain down from the parapet above as the assailants make for a protrusion of masonry level with the second tier of casemates in the largely destroyed fort. Only 11 out of a total of 25 Navy boats managed to land men at the fort. Of approximately 400 Marines and sailors who volunteered for the action, eight were killed, 19 wounded, and 105 captured. Fort Sumter continued to defy Union forces until February 17, 1865, when it was abandoned as Confederate forces withdrew from Charleston.

First Lieutenant Charles H. Bradford, USMC, died of wounds received during the assault on Fort Sumter, September 8, 1863. (Naval History and Heritage Command, NH 56225)

opposing Sherman. Using all the disposable troops in his department, Foster collected about 5,500 men in what was unofficially designated the Coast Division, and delegated command of the expedition to Brigadier General John P. Hatch.

Composed of about 350 sailors plus 157 Marines from ships of the South Atlantic Blockading Squadron, under the overall authority of Commander George H. Preble, the Marine component of the Fleet Brigade was under First Lieutenant (acting Lieutenant Colonel) George G. Stoddard, commander of the Marine Guard aboard the store ship *New Hampshire*.

The sailors were organized as a battalion each of artillery and infantry, commanded by Lieutenant Commander Edmund O. Matthews and Lieutenant James O'Kane respectively, while the Marines were formed into a three-company battalion of skirmishers with a sergeant fulfilling the role of captain for each small company. Following several days of training in battalion drill at Bay Point, on Edisto Island, South Carolina, the Fleet Brigade embarked on the gunboats *Sonoma*, *Mingoe*, and *Pontiac* on November 29, and under cover of dense fog entered the Broad River, about 30 miles down the coast. Penetrating inland about 20 miles, the flotilla steamed up a creek south of Boyd's Neck, South Carolina.

Disembarking from *Sonoma* in ship's boats at 0900hrs, the Marines quickly deployed as skirmishers and proceeded toward Grahamville, with the battalion of sailor infantry marching in column and the naval artillerists bringing up the rear pulling two four-gun batteries of boat-howitzers. Troops of the Coast Division landed at the same place and proceeded as the main body of the expedition. Advancing rapidly inland, the Fleet Brigade made several wrong turns due to inaccurate maps and eventually joined forces with the Coast Division near Bolan Church, South Carolina, at the junction of the Honey Hill and River roads, where they entrenched and bivouacked for the night.

An advance on the Charleston and Savannah Railroad was ordered the next morning but after marching about 6 miles the expedition encountered and engaged with Confederates near Honey Hill. Two companies of the battalion of sailor infantry took turns on the drag ropes to bring the boat-howitzers into action. Observing the moment, a newspaper reporter with the expedition wrote later: "When the order came ... to go to the front and take position on the right, a hundred or two brawny hands were thrust into blue shirts for tobacco, and a hundred cheeks protruded ... and then they went ahead, led by the sturdy Commander Preble, his grey hair fluttering in the breeze" (*DST*, December 15, 1864: 2.2).

Initially also held in reserve, the Marines, accompanied by the African-American 55th Massachusetts Infantry of the Coast Division, were ordered forward to relieve the right of the Union line. The Marines advanced through nearly 1 mile of thick woods and swamp before going into line of battle on the double-quick. For the next three hours, they engaged with Confederate infantry and artillery, while battalion acting Quartermaster-Sergeant Jeremiah Cogley braved heavy enemy fire to keep his men supplied with ammunition from the rear. Around 1400hrs, Acting Ensign Woodward Carter, USN, who was serving as acting major of the battalion, took 20 Marines to reconnoiter the Confederate left flank but soon returned having observed that the enemy force at their front was too strong to break through. Thus, the whole Expeditionary Force was ordered to withdraw that evening. Despite the length of the engagement of the Fleet Brigade at Honey Hill, the day's fighting had left just one killed, six wounded, and 14 men missing (*ORNs*, I.16: 77).

Two further unsuccessful attempts were made to cut the Charleston and Savannah Railroad on December 5–6, 1864, via the Tulifinny River, following which the Fleet Brigade was stood down and the sailors and Marines were returned to their respective vessels in the South Atlantic Blockading Squadron.

Commander Foxhall A. Parker, USN commanded the Fleet Brigade created on July 12, 1863. A Navy veteran, he was first appointed a midshipman in 1837, and later served aboard USS *Constitution* under his father Foxhall A. Parker, Sr. Commissioned a lieutenant in 1850, he saw action in the Third Seminole War (1855–58), and served on the Great Lakes, in the Mediterranean, and in the Pacific Ocean. With the outbreak of the Civil War he was appointed executive officer at the Navy Yard in Washington, DC, where he drilled about 2,000 sailors in the exercise of artillery and small arms in preparation for their service with the Western Gunboat Flotilla, which later became the Mississippi River Squadron. On December 31, 1863, he took command of the large Potomac Flotilla until the end of the war. (Naval History and Heritage Command, NH 47408)

FORT FISHER, DECEMBER 23, 1864–JANUARY 15, 1865

Nicknamed the Gibraltar of the Confederacy, Fort Fisher was a formidable bastion commanding the Cape Fear River in North Carolina. Commanded by Colonel William Lamb, the fort encompassed 14,500 square feet and was surrounded by a 10ft parapet and network of bombproofs, most of which were 30ft high. Obstructions forming its outer defenses included land mines or torpedoes, abattis, and deep ditches. Since 1861 the fort had protected the vital trading routes of the port at Wilmington, North Carolina, which by the winter of 1864 was the last Confederate port open to blockade runners. The capture of Fort Fisher would sever that link and ring the death knell for the Confederacy.

In December 1864, Major General Benjamin Butler, commanding the Department of Virginia and North Carolina, and the Army of the James, devised a plan to breach the defenses of Fort Fisher by exploding a ship loaded with gunpowder against its sea-facing walls, following which troops would be landed to storm the breach. In conjunction with Rear Admiral David D. Porter, commanding the North Atlantic Blockading Squadron, Lieutenant General Ulysses S. Grant approved the plan, but assigned Major General Godfrey Weitzel to lead the assault force, despite Butler being in command of the department. Exercising command discretion, Butler chose to join the expedition off the coast of Fort Fisher aboard the Army steamboat *Charles Chamberlain*, flagship of Graham's Naval Brigade, and personally take charge of the operation.

Meanwhile, Grant was unaware that Confederate spies at Hampton Roads had reported specific intelligence about ship and troop movements to Richmond, which prompted General Robert E. Lee to send the division of Major General Robert F. Hoke, composed of about 6,500 veteran troops, from the Richmond–Petersburg lines, to reinforce Fort Fisher.

Butler's plan was to bring the steamer *Louisiana*, packed with 200 tons of gunpowder and disguised as a blockade runner, south from Fortress Monroe to Fort Fisher, tow the vessel about 100yd from the latter fort's seawall, and blow *Louisiana* up, possibly demolishing part of the fort as well. Following this, troops would be landed several miles north along the beach after a naval bombardment.

Despite Butler's troop transports being delayed at Beaufort, North Carolina, due to a storm, Porter began the bombardment on December 23 and decided to explode *Louisiana*, which was too far off the shore to have any effect on Fort Fisher. The troop transports arrived that evening and, despite the failure of the Navy to weaken the defenses of Fort Fisher, decided to land a reconnaissance party to determine if an attack might still be feasible. Under the direct command of Weitzel, the landings began on Christmas Day morning, with the Second Division, XXIV Army Corps, commanded by Brigadier General Adelbert Ames, as the first ashore.

Weitzel pushed down the peninsula, capturing several small outposts along the way and scouting the approaches to Fort Fisher. Halting, he deployed his main force about 800yd from the base of the fort to evaluate the situation. An advance force of about 500 skirmishers probed the fort's north-facing defenses, with unsatisfactory results. Following this, the Confederate defenders repulsed the Union line with canister and musket fire from strong

OPPOSITE
Published in *The Soldier in our Civil War*, Vol. 2, in 1890, this chart by Walter A. Lane shows the positions and lines of fire of 58 vessels of the Union Navy fleet under Rear Admiral David D. Porter during the second attack on Fort Fisher, North Carolina, on January 13–15, 1865. (Naval History and Heritage Command NH 59170)

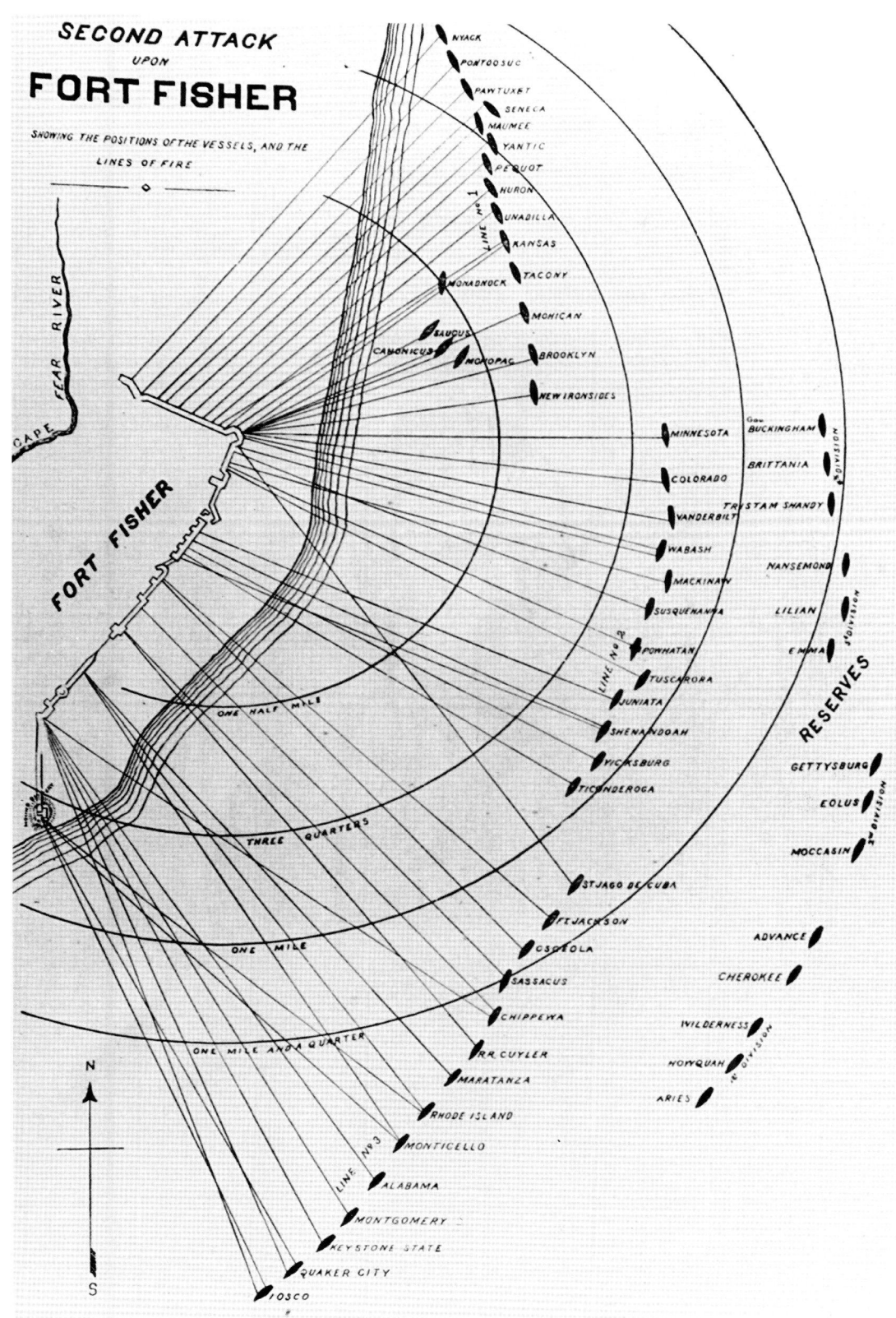

SECOND ATTACK
UPON
FORT FISHER

SHOWING THE POSITIONS OF THE VESSELS, AND THE
LINES OF FIRE

CAPE FEAR RIVER

FORT FISHER

NYACK
PONTOOSUC
PAWTUXET
SENECA
MAUMEE
YANTIC
PEQUOT
HURON
UNADILLA
KANSAS
TACONY
MONADNOCK
SAUGUS
MOHICAN
CANONICUS
MONOPAC
BROOKLYN
NEW IRONSIDES

LINE No 1

MINNESOTA
COLORADO
VANDERBILT
WABASH
MACKINAW
SUSQUEHANNA
POWHATAN
TUSCARORA
JUNIATA
SHENANDOAH
VICKSBURG
TICONDEROGA

LINE No 2

ST JAGO DE CUBA
F.E. JACKSON
OSCEOLA
SASSACUS
CHIPPEWA
R.R. CUYLER
MARATANZA
RHODE ISLAND
MONTICELLO
ALABAMA
MONTGOMERY
KEYSTONE STATE
QUAKER CITY
IOSCO

LINE No 3

GOV. BUCKINGHAM
BRITTANIA
TRYSTAM SHANDY
NANSEMOND
LILIAN
E MMA
GETTYSBURG
EOLUS
MOCCASIN

RESERVES

ADVANCE
CHEROKEE
WILDERNESS
HOWQUAH
ARIES

1ST DIVISION
2D DIVISION
3D DIVISION
4TH DIVISION

ONE HALF MILE
THREE QUARTERS
ONE MILE
ONE MILE AND A QUARTER

N

S

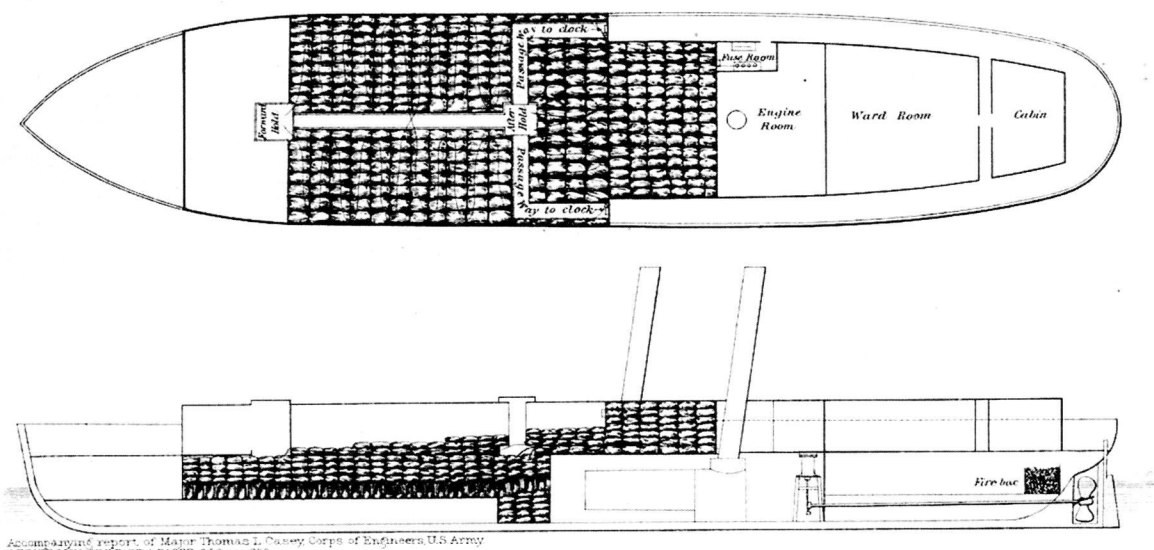

Accompanying report, of Major Thomas L. Casey Corps of Engineers, U.S. Army
SERIES I VOL. XLII PART 1 PAGES 989 AND 990

positions, causing much doubt in Weitzel's mind about the success of the operation. Ordering a boat to row him out to *Charles Chamberlain*, he conferred with Butler and explained that an assault on Fort Fisher under the present circumstances would lead to the slaughter of his troops. Butler concurred and ordered the landing force to disengage and re-embark.

Meanwhile the weather worsened and a rough sea made re-embarkation difficult. By 2300hrs the operation had to be suspended and, as at Hatteras Inlet some three years earlier, Butler left cold and hungry troops stranded on an enemy-occupied beach overnight. During the next day, elements of the Naval Battalion aboard *Charles Chamberlain* stretched a hawser between their vessel and the shore, and managed to bring off a few men in launches and other small craft that were sometimes dangerously close to being swamped by the turbulent sea. A newspaper correspondent with the expedition later reported: "The shore is strewn with broken boats, mostly naval, which have been wrecked in one way or another. They lie strewn along the beach from Fort Fisher to Masonboro Inlet" (*PI*, January 2, 1865: 1.3). The wind finally shifted to offshore and moderated the sea on December 27 and, after rigging two more hawsers from ship to shore, the Naval Battalion was able to rescue the remaining troops by about 1300hrs, following which the combined Union fleet returned to Fortress Monroe.

Butler's mismanagement of a second amphibious operation led to his recall to Washington, DC, in early 1865. As Secretary of War Stanton was not

G UNION ARMY TRANSPORT STEAMER, 1864

This transport steamer was built under supervision of Norman Wiard at the Continental Iron Works at Greenpoint, Brooklyn, New York City. Its overall length was 160ft, while the breadth of beam was 21ft 4in. Being double-ended with two pilothouses (**1**) and a shallow draft (30in when loaded and 22in when lightened), it was designed to negotiate and penetrate the narrow inlets and rivers of the southern coast without the need to turn round.

The steamer had bulkheads (**2**) at both ends, two engines (**3**), four boilers, a central smokestack (**4**), and paddle wheels (**5**) 16ft in diameter. On the main deck, there were six guns on sliding carriages (**6**) and two launches (**7**); spars (**8**) were placed fore and aft with geared winches (**9**) for hoisting launches, guns, and horses on and off the vessel.

On the promenade deck were the officers' quarters (**10**) and a messroom (**11**). There was a portable way and stepladder (**12**) to connect the promenade deck to the main deck when the launches were on board. Between decks were the men's quarters, kitchen (**13**), store room (**14**), stalls for 30 horses (**15**), and water closets (**16**).

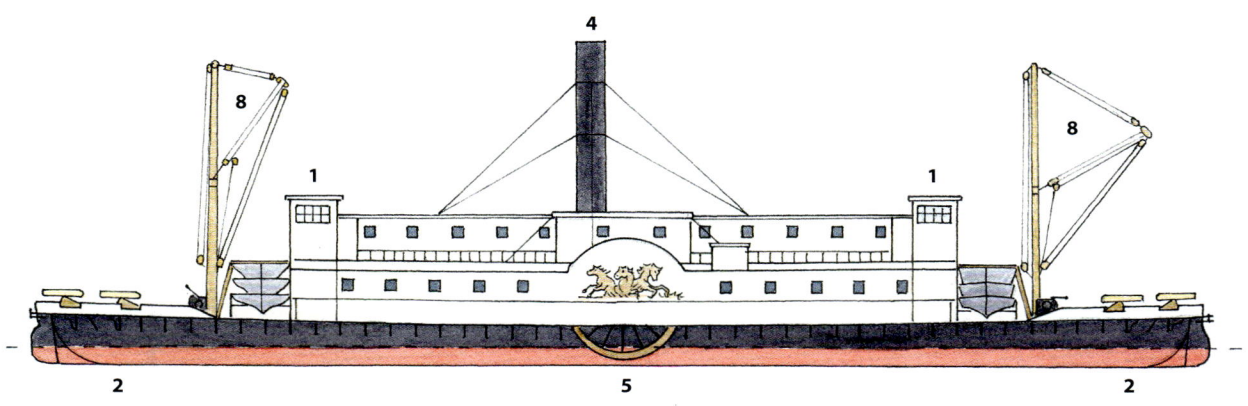

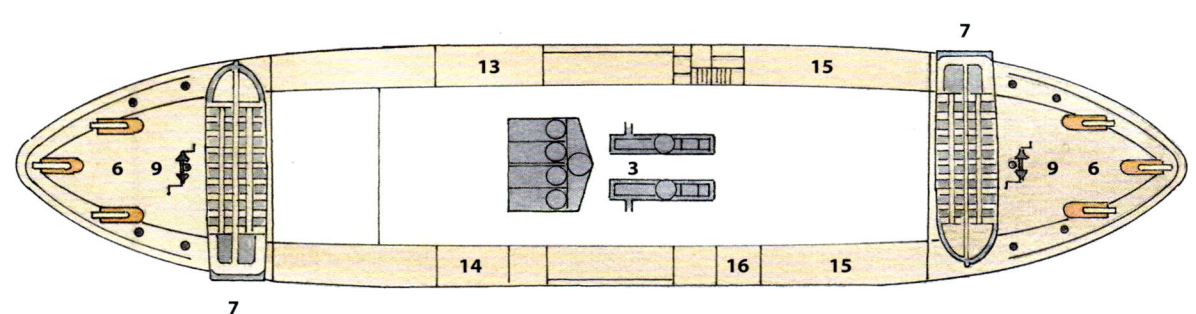

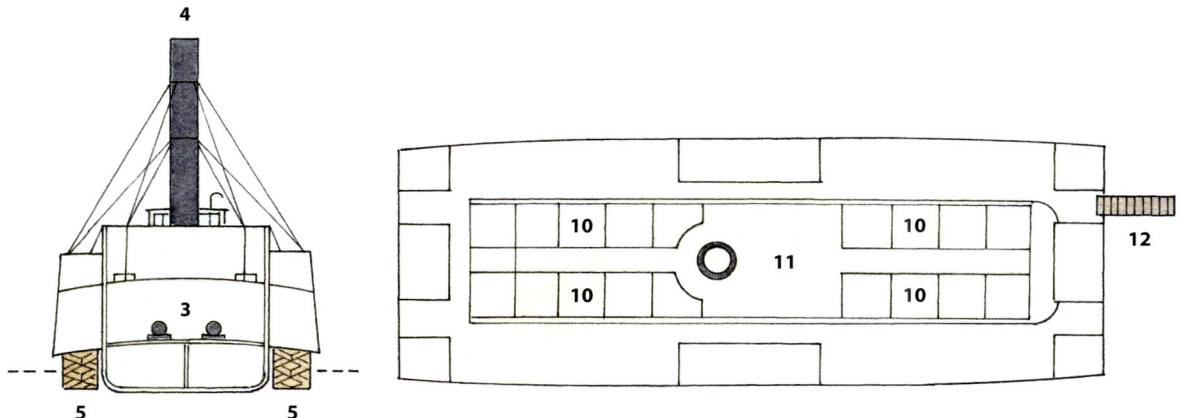

J.W. Grattan.

FORT FISHER

in the capital at that time, Grant appealed directly to President Lincoln for permission to terminate Butler's appointment. This resulted in General Order No. 1, which relieved him of command on January 8, 1865, following which Grant named Major General Edward O.C. Ord to replace him as commander of the Department of Virginia and North Carolina, and Army of the James.

Intent on ensuring that a second attack on Fort Fisher would succeed, Grant did not advise his new expedition commander, Major General Alfred H. Terry, of his destination until Rear Admiral Porter's fleet, plus Army transports, had put to sea from Fortress Monroe on January 11, 1865, when sealed orders were opened explaining the mission. He also permitted information to be leaked that Terry and his force were to join Sherman's army in Savannah, thereby providing a plausible explanation for all the naval activity.

On January 13, 1865, the lone side-wheel gunboat *Tacony* arrived off Fort Fisher at about 0500hrs with lights ablaze to serve as a beacon, or steering point, for Porter's fleet. The rest of the fleet arrived at about 0700hrs, and formed into three main battle lines. About 1 mile north of the fort, Line No. 1 consisted of 14 gunboats of various classes and four ironclads. Line No. 2, composed of 12 more gunboats, was directly opposite the fort. South of the fort, Line No. 3 was made up of a further 12 gunboats. Behind Lines 2 and 3 were 17 smaller gunboats formed into four reserve divisions. Serving as Porter's flagship, the side-wheel steamer *Malvern* was north of Line No. 2 and almost level with the reserve divisions. Behind Line No. 1 came 19 Army transport steamers carrying 8,000 troops of the XXIV and XXV corps. Including tenders and tugboats, the whole expedition consisted of about 80 vessels.

At 0715hrs the gunboats in Line No. 1 "beat to quarters" and opened fire on the narrow strip of woods beyond the beach to the north of Fort Fisher in preparation for the troop landings (NARA, RG 24: Log of USS *Yantic*, p. 83, right). At 0820hrs, *New Ironsides* led the ironclads *Monadnock*, *Saugus*, *Canonicus*, and *Mahopac* in front of Line No. 1 and took up position about 700yd from the fort. These formidable vessels opened fire on the fort's northeast-facing walls at about 0830hrs. At about the same time, all ships in the fleet were signaled to send boats to the Army transports to assist in disembarking troops in preparation for the landings. Describing what followed next, a newspaper correspondent with the expedition wrote:

> The transports were enabled to go within half a mile of the shore, and they were soon surrounded by not less than 200 boats, supplied from all the vessels of the fleet. Several tugs also joined in the work, and carried the soldiers to within 100 yards of the beach, where they were transferred to small boats. The tents and camp equipage were also landed, with several days' provisions for the entire force, 8,000 strong, at 9 o'clock. The boats from all the transports moved for the shore, and in a few minutes the first 500 men stepped on the beach and planted their regimental flag on one of the highest sand-hills, amid cheering from the transports and the fleet. (*SEP*, January 26, 1865: 3.2)

The first boat to land contained men of the 169th New York Infantry, under Lieutenant Colonel James A. Colvin. Although the sea was relatively calm, easterly winds caused the waves to break with considerable force along the shore. Some of the boats carried small kedge anchors and a hawser that they dropped outside the surf, enabling them to reach the beach stern-first.

In many cases the troops jumped into the waist-deep water, and some of these fell and were thoroughly immersed, soaking knapsacks and ammunition.

The troops were soon formed up and marched to within 2½ miles of Fort Fisher, where they entrenched until morning. According to a newspaper correspondent aboard the Army hospital ship *Blackstone*, "Camp fires blazed all along the beach for four or five miles, which, with the myriad lights of the fleet," created "one of the most impressive ... sights of the war" (*NYDT*, January 19, 1865: 1.6).

More troops, plus artillery, were landed the next day, including Major General Terry whose headquarters was established on the advanced line facing Fort Fisher. Meanwhile breastworks were thrown up across the peninsula from the sea coast to the bank of the Cape Fear River facing Wilmington. Preparations were made for a general assault on Fort Fisher to take place at 1500hrs on January 15. Moving into position at 0130hrs with the right flank of the Second Division, XXIV Corps, Army of the James, resting on the Cape Fear River, Lieutenant Colonel Samuel M. Zent led 60 sharpshooters of the 13th Indiana Infantry, armed with Spencer repeating rifles, ahead of Brevet Brigadier General Newton M. Curtis's 1st Brigade, composed of the 112th, 117th, 42d, and 3d New York Infantry. The 2d Brigade, consisting of the 47th, 48th, 76th, and 203d Pennsylvania Infantry, took up position in the center about 0200hrs. The left flank was to consist of the sailors and Marines of the fleet once they had landed later that day.

Prior to the commencement of the bombardment on January 13, the executive officer of every Navy vessel involved in the expedition was ordered by Porter to detail as many of the men as possible from the guns as a landing party, that the Navy may have "a share in the assault when it takes place"

Based on a painting by Alonzo Chappel (1828–87), this lithograph shows the orderly landing of troops on the beach during the bombardment of Fort Fisher on January 15, 1865. As the soldiers assemble on the beach, sailors row back out to the troop transports to collect more men. (Naval History and Heritage Command NH 2007)

(*SEP*, January 26, 1865: 3.3). In preparation for this, boats were to be kept ready, lowered near the water, on the off side of each vessel. The sailors were to be armed with cutlasses and revolvers. Those who had served in the Army were issued Sharps New Model 1863 Rifles. When the signal was given, the men were to man the boats and pull around the stern of their vessel and land in preparation for the assault in a "seaman-like way" (*SEP*, January 26, 1865: 3.3). Upon landing, the order concluded, "The Marines will form in the rear and cover the sailors, whilst the soldiers are going at the parapet in front. Sailors will take the sea-face of Fort Fisher" (*SEP*, January 26, 1865: 3.2–3).

Aboard the side-wheel gunboat *Santiago de Cuba*, Captain Oliver S. Glisson informed the crew that he wanted 35 volunteers and all that could be spared from the guns. Volunteers were invited to advance to the port side of the vessel. Following a "pretty general rush" to the port side, Glisson stopped them, having 38 more men than required. A correspondent of the *Philadelphia Inquirer* aboard the ship concluded his report by stating: "At the time I write, the grindstone is at work sharpening cutlasses, and the storming party evince as much gleesome hilarity as a party of children preparing for a pic-nic. The same spirit has been manifested on all the vessels, and if Fort Fisher is not taken there will at least be some bloody work" (*PI*, January 18, 1865: 8.2).

Leaving their respective vessels at 1100hrs on January 15, 1,600 sailors and 400 Marines landed on the beach and were organized into three divisions under overall command of Lieutenant Commander Kidder R. Breese, while the Marines were under direct command of Captain Lucian L. Dawson, the senior Marine officer of the fleet. Formed into a column, the sailors and Marines advanced toward the sea-facing northeast corner of Fort Fisher, while the Army approached the northwest corner.

This watercolor by Ensign John W. Grattan depicts the storming of Fort Fisher on January 15, 1865, with the bombarding fleet positioned offshore. Flying signal flags, Rear Admiral Porter's flagship *Malvern* is at center. The ironclad *New Ironsides* and the monitors are at the right. (Naval History and Heritage Command NH 50467-KN)

J.W. Grattan.

At 1500hrs, the signal was given and the general attack began. As the sailors sprang up and charged, the guns of the great Mound Battery and Half-Moon Battery in Fort Fisher opened up in their front and flank. The attack plan involved the Marines hastily digging rifle pits from which to offer covering fire as the sailors advanced, but according to Lieutenant Commander Thomas O. Selfridge, Jr., who commanded the Third Naval Division, it was "impossible to dig such shelter trenches near enough to do much good in broad daylight" (Selfridge 1888: 659). Hence, the attack took place without effective covering fire. Watching the action from the deck of *Santiago de Cuba*, a newspaper correspondent wrote:

> In an instant the naval brigade on the beach was observed moving forward toward the front. They had about a mile to go to reach the abattis. They had scarcely got in motion before shells from the mound and water batteries were poured upon them. Numbers of them were seen to fall, and scores of others to start back, limping or crawling on their hands and knees. Onward, however, the main body pressed at a double-quick, the fire momentarily increasing in its fatal effects. Until the whole line of beach over which they had travelled was strewn with dead and wounded. Some had fallen so near the rolling surf that their bodies could be seen tossing up and down the beach with the advancing tide. The ditch and abattis was about one hundred yards from the ramparts, and into this they poured until it was filled to overflowing, when two guns were opened upon them with grape and canister from the ramparts, tearing the abattis in front of them and adding largely to their casualties. The rebel gunboats Chickamauga and Lilian were also shelling them from Cape Fear river, and altogether it was a moment of

Published in *Deeds of Valor*, Vol. II, in 1907, this lithograph depicts an advance party of Marines who volunteered to take up an advanced position to offer covering fire during the assault on Fort Fisher conducted by sailors of the Fleet Naval Brigade. Pinned down by bursting shells and a hail of musket balls, and musketry, they maintained their post until nightfall permitted them to return unscathed to their lines. Sergeant Richard D. Binder and other surviving members of this party were awarded the Medal of Honor. (Naval History and Heritage Command NH 79938)

Although mainly armed with cutlasses and revolvers, most sailors of the Fleet Naval Brigade did not get close enough to the Confederate defenders to use these weapons. Coming under heavy shellfire and musketry, about 60 of them were forced to seek shelter behind the abattis about 200ft from the main enemy earthworks, while the remainder withdrew behind the sand hills. This illustration was published in 1888 in *Battles and Leaders of the Civil War*. (Author's collection)

frightful interest. It soon became evident that these gallant men must retire or all be sacrificed. (*TP*, January 19, 1865: 1.4)

About 200 naval officers and men had managed to reach the abattis that stretched down to the beach. Leading the Second Division, Lieutenant Commander James Parker, Jr., recalled: "For some cause or other, the mass of the sailors ... had halted nearly a quarter of a mile to the northward and laid down under cover of the crest of the beach" (*ORNs*, I.11: 496). At the head of the Third Division, Lieutenant Commander Selfridge observed:

Seaman David L. Bass proudly posed for this photograph wearing the Medal of Honor he received in June 1865 for bravery during the second attack on Fort Fisher. One of 40 sailors acknowledged for their bravery during the assault, he advanced to the top of the sand hill and partly through a breach in the palisade in the defenses of the fort despite many of those around him being killed or wounded. (US National Archives

Serving as a flag-lieutenant to Rear Admiral Porter, Samuel W. Preston participated in the attacks on Fort Fisher on December 24–25, 1864, and January 15, 1865. Born to American parents residing in Ontario, Canada in 1842, Preston was appointed midshipman from the state of Illinois on October 4, 1858. Graduating from the Naval Academy first in his class on May 9, 1861, he was appointed acting master on October 4, 1861, and lieutenant on August 1, 1862. He was assigned as flag-lieutenant under Rear Admiral Samuel F. Du Pont, and chief of staff for Rear Admiral John A. Dahlgren in 1863. Captured by Confederate forces while leading a storming party during the attack on Fort Sumter that year, he was imprisoned for 14 months in the Richland County Jail in Columbia, South Carolina, until exchanged during the fall of 1864. Ordered to the North Atlantic Blockading Squadron as flag-lieutenant to Rear Admiral David D. Porter, he was killed when a fragment of exploding shell struck his abdomen during the amphibious assault on Fort Fisher in January 1865. (Naval History and Heritage Command NH 47236)

Published by Currier & Ives, c.1865–72, this lithograph depicts the Union Army assault under Major General Alfred H. Terry on the northwest corner of Fort Fisher on January 15, 1865. The ironclads and frigates of Rear Admiral Porter's fleet are shown pouring a destructive fire of shot and shell into the fortifications. The original description accompanying this print concluded, "Three cheers for the Army and Navy!" (LOC LC-DIG-ppmsca-35358)

Though many dropped rapidly under this fire, the column never faltered, and when the angle where the two faces of the fort unite was reached the head halted to allow the rear to come up. This halt was fatal, for as the others came up they followed suit and lay down till the space between the parapet and the edge of the water was filled. (Selfridge 1888: 659)

Urging those with him to advance farther up a sand hill toward Fort Fisher and through a breach in the palisade, Parker turned and saw that only about 60 men had followed him. The rest had panicked and retreated at a run. Lacking adequate training and preparation for land battle, the volunteer sailors found great difficulty in standing up to veteran Confederate troops armed with rifled muskets.

Meanwhile, the Army became involved in a bitter struggle to seize the rest of the northward-facing defenses of Fort Fisher and finally, by 2200hrs, broke through and forced a Confederate surrender. With musketry fire now concentrated on his remaining sailors, Parker ordered them to take cover behind the abattis. There they remained until dark when they slipped back to their own lines taking their wounded, arms, and colors with them. Although unsuccessful in its specific objective, the naval assault drew a large proportion of the enemy to the northeast corner of the fort, leaving only about 250 of the Confederate garrison to defend the Cape Fear River end of the works against the assault of Major General Ames' Division, 24th Army Corps. This ensured the Union victory and capture of approximately 1,900 Confederates, 75 large-caliber guns, and Major General William H.C. Whiting. During the naval attack, 82 sailors and Marines were killed, 269 wounded, and 35 listed as missing.

H BRAVERY AT THE PALISADE, FORT FISHER, JANUARY 15, 1865

Commanding the Second Division of sailors during the naval assault on Fort Fisher, Lieutenant Commander James Parker, Jr., led his men beyond the abatis at the foot of the defense works of the fort on January 15, 1865. Giving the order to advance, he waved his sword and started climbing up the steep slope of the Confederate earthworks followed by about 60 men who remained with him. Meanwhile, others had been seized with panic and were retreating on the run despite efforts to rally them. Finding the Confederates were concentrating their fire on his men with musket balls zipping all around them, Parker ordered them to take shelter behind the palisade, following which he joined them. Remaining there until nightfall, the Union sailors managed to slip back to their own lines before the Confederate surrender, bringing their wounded with them. These were some of the 40 sailors, six Marines, and eight soldiers who were eventually awarded the Medal of Honor for brave conduct during the action on January 15, 1865.

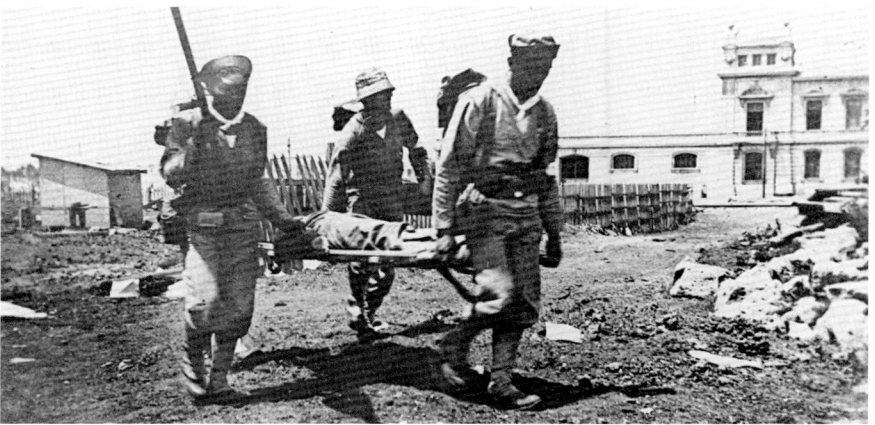

Sailors from USS *Florida* serve as stretcher-bearers in Veracruz, Mexico, in 1914. US forces conducted an amphibious landing and seized the Mexican port city on April 21, 1914, and held it until their withdrawal on November 23 that year. Photograph courtesy of R.V. Hanberry Jr. AMC, USN (Ret.). (Naval History and Heritage Command, NH 123378)

CONCLUSION

Amphibious tactics employed by the Union Army and Navy during the Civil War had developed considerably by January 1865. In terms of combined operations, both services had learned much about the coordination and control of men and vessels in the unpredictable environment along the sea coast and Western Rivers. Specialist units such as the 1st New York Marine Artillery and the Naval Battalion, 13th New York Heavy Artillery, successfully penetrated inland along the rivers in specially built shallow-draught steamers and launches using highly mobile guns developed by John Dahlgren and Norman Wiard.

Although they did not represent pure amphibious actions in the classical, blue-water sense, the innovative riverine tactics of the Mississippi Marine Brigade helped control the Confederate guerrilla threat along the Western Rivers. By 1863, Dahlgren had created a naval brigade consisting of Union Navy sailors and Marines, which, in conjunction with the Army, achieved ultimate success with the fall of Fort Fisher on January 15, 1865.

The beach-landing tactics developed by all of these means during the Civil War formed a foundation for those implemented 80 years later in the European and Pacific theaters of World War II. Likewise, tactics pioneered on the Western Rivers by Alfred W. Ellet and his Mississippi Marine Brigade were further developed by the Mobile Riverine Force during the Vietnam conflict of the 1960s and 1970s.

SELECT BIBLIOGRAPHY

Abraham Lincoln papers: Series 1. General Correspondence. 1833 to 1916: Winfield Scott to Abraham Lincoln, Thursday, Report on George B. McClellan's letter of April 27, 1861 to Scott. May 2, 1861. Washington, DC: Library of Congress.

Avery, William B. (1880). *The Marine Artillery with the Burnside Expedition and the Battle of Camden, N.C.* Providence, RI: N. Bangs Williams & Co., Personal Narratives of Events in the War of Rebellion, Being Papers Read Before the Rhode Island Soldiers and Sailors Historical Society, No. 4, Second Series, p.9.

Browning, Robert M. Jr. (1993). *From Cape Charles to Cape Fear: The North Atlantic Blockading Squadron during the Civil War.* Tuscaloosa, AL: University of Alabama Press.

Crandall, Warren T., & Isaac D. Newell (1907). *History of the Ram Fleet and the Mississippi Marine Brigade*. St. Louis, MO: Press of Buschart Bros.

Dahlgren, Captain John A. (1852). *Form of Exercise and Manœuvre for the Boat-Howitzers of the U.S. Navy*. Washington, DC: Government Printing Office.

Dahlgren, Lieutenant John A. (1852). *System of Boat Armament in the United States Navy*. Philadelphia, PA: printed by A. Hart, 126 Chestnut Street.

Dahlgren, Madeleine Vinton (1892). *Memoir of John A. Dahlgren. Rear-Admiral United States Navy*. Boston, MA: James R. Osgood & Co.

Daniel O'Connor Letters, Collection 429, Folder 1, Letter dated September 18, 1861, Archives Branch, History Division, Marine Corps Historical Center, Quantico, VA 22134.

Documents of the Assembly of the State of New-York (1863). Eighty-sixth Session. Albany, NY: Comstock & Cassidy, Printers.

Graham, Lieutenant Matthew J. (1900). *The Ninth Regiment New York Volunteers (Hawkins' Zouaves)*. New York, NY: E.F. Coby & Co.

Hayes, John D. & Lillian O'Brien, eds (1962). "The Early Blockade and the Capture of the Hatteras Forts," *The New-York Historical Society Quarterly*. January, Vol. XLVI, No. 1: 61–85.

Hewett, Janet B. et al., ed. (1994–2001). *Supplement to the Official Records of the Union and Confederate Armies*. Wilmington, NC: Broadfoot Publishing Co. See *SOR*s, Part, Volume, Page.

National Archives & Records Administration. M-1281, Ordnance Quarterly Returns, Roll 4, 356; Roll 2, 217–219; & Roll 1, 338–347.

National Archives & Records Administration, Record Group 24: Records of the Bureau of Naval Personnel: Logbooks of U.S. Navy Ships, *c*.1801–1940, Log of USS *Yantic*.

Selfridge, Jr., Captain Thomas O., USN (1888). "The Navy at Fort Fisher," *Battles and Leaders of the Civil War*. New York, NY: The Century Co.

Symonds, Craig L. (2010). *Union Combined Operations in the Civil War*. New York, NY: Fordham University Press.

United States Naval War Records Office, and United States Office of Naval Records and Library. *Official Records of the Union and Confederate Navies in the War of the Rebellion*. Harrisburg, PA: National Historical Society, 1987. See *ORN*s, Series, Volume, Page.

United States War Records Office, et al. *The War of the Rebellion: a Compilation of the Official Records of the Union and Confederate Armies*. Washington, DC: Government Printing Office, 1880–1901. See *OR*s, Series, Volume, Part, Page.

Whitney, John H.E. (1866). *The Hawkins' Zouaves: (Ninth N.Y.V.) Their Battles and Marches*. New York, NY: Published by the author.

Wiard, Norman (1863). *Marine Artillery as Adapted for Service on the Coast and on Inland Waters*. New York, NY: Holman, Printer, Corner and White Streets.

Newspapers

Bangor Daily Whig and Courier, Bangor, ME (*BDWC*); *Boston Recorder*, Boston, MA (*BR*); *Boston Semi-Weekly Advertiser*, Boston, MA (*BSWA*); *Brooklyn Daily Eagle*, New York City, NY (*BDE*); *Chicago Daily Tribune*, Chicago, IL (*CDT*); *Chicago Tribune*, Chicago, IL (*CT*); *Chicago Weekly Tribune*, Chicago. IL (*CWT*); *Daily Democrat and News*, Davenport, IA (*DDN*); *Daily Evening Express*, Lancaster City, PA (*DEE*); *Daily Evening Standard*, New Bedford, MA (*DES*); *Daily Missouri Republican*, St. Louis, MO (*DMR*); *Daily Ohio Statesman*, Columbus, OH (*DOS*); *Daily Sentinel and Times*, Bath, ME (*DST*); *Evening Press*, Providence, RI (*EP*); *Evening Star*, Washington, DC (*ES*); *Lutheran Observer*, Baltimore, MD (*LO*); *Memphis Bulletin*, Memphis, TN (*MB*); *Newbern Weekly Progress*, New Bern, NC (*NWP*); *New-London Daily Chronicle*, New London, CT (*NLDC*); *New York Daily Herald*, New York City, NY (*NYDH*); *New York Daily Tribune*, New York City, NY (*NYDT*); *New York Illustrated News*, New York City, NY (*NYIN*); *New York Times*, New York City, NY (*NYT*); *New-York Semi-Weekly Tribune*, New York City, NY (*NYSWT*); *Philadelphia Inquirer*, Philadelphia, PA (*PI*); *Saint Paul Weekly Minnesotian*, St. Paul, MN (*SPWM*); *Saturday Evening Press*, Menasha, WI (*SEP*); *The Daily Age*, Philadelphia, PA (*TDA*); *The Press*, Philadelphia, PA (*TP*); *The World*, New York City, NY (*TW*); *Washington Democrat*, Salem, IN (*WD*); *West-Jersey Pioneer*, Bridgeton, NJ (*WJP*).

INDEX

References to illustrations are shown in **bold**. Plates are shown with page locators in brackets.